Project Management Institute

D1109021

Project Manager Competency Development (PMCD) Framework
Second Edition

ISBN 13: 978-1-933890-34-0
ISBN 10: 1-933890-34-7

Published by:
  Project Management Institute, Inc.
  14 Campus Boulevard
  Newtown Square, Pennsylvania 19073-3299 USA.
  Phone: +1-610-356-4600
  Fax: +1-610-356-4647
  E-mail: customercare@pmi.org

Internet: www.pmi.org

To inquire about discounts for resale or educational purposes, please contact the PMI Book Service Center.
  PMI Book Service Center
  P.O. Box 932683, Atlanta, GA 31193-2683 USA
  Phone: 1-866-276-4764 (within the U.S. or Canada) or +1-770-280-4129 (globally)
  Fax: +1-770-280-4113
  E-mail: book.orders@pmi.org

10 9 8 7 6 5 4 3 2

Notice

The Project Management Institute, Inc. (PMI) standards and guideline publications, of which the document contained herein is one, are developed through a voluntary consensus standards development process. This process brings together volunteers and/or seeks out the views of persons who have an interest in the topic covered by this publication. While PMI administers the process and establishes rules to promote fairness in the development of consensus, it does not write the document and it does not independently test, evaluate, or verify the accuracy or completeness of any information or the soundness of any judgments contained in its standards and guideline publications.

PMI disclaims liability for any personal injury, property or other damages of any nature whatsoever, whether special, indirect, consequential or compensatory, directly or indirectly resulting from the publication, use of application, or reliance on this document. PMI disclaims and makes no guaranty or warranty, expressed or implied, as to the accuracy or completeness of any information published herein, and disclaims and makes no warranty that the information in this document will fulfill any of your particular purposes or needs. PMI does not undertake to guarantee the performance of any individual manufacturer or seller's products or services by virtue of this standard or guide.

In publishing and making this document available, PMI is not undertaking to render professional or other services for or on behalf of any person or entity, nor is PMI undertaking to perform any duty owed by any person or entity to someone else. Anyone using this document should rely on his or her own independent judgment or, as appropriate, seek the advice of a competent professional in determining the exercise of reasonable care in any given circumstances. Information and other standards on the topic covered by this publication may be available from other sources, which the user may wish to consult for additional views or information not covered by this publication.

PMI has no power, nor does it undertake to police or enforce compliance with the contents of this document. PMI does not certify, test, or inspect products, designs, or installations for safety or health purposes. Any certification or other statement of compliance with any health or safety-related information in this document shall not be attributable to PMI and is solely the responsibility of the certifier or maker of the statement.

Contents

List of Tables and Figures

Preface to the Second Edition

This standard builds upon the framework developed in the *Project Management Competency Development Framework* published in 2002. When the project team was launched in early 2004, the Project Management Institute was finalizing a large research project to support the PMP® certification process. The outcome of that role delineation study was the *PMP® Examination Specification.* The research showed that the project management industry viewed projects from a *process* perspective rather than a *Knowledge Area* view.

The *PMCD Framework* project team was asked, as a result, to provide a revised document that accomplished the following:

- Tightly aligned the *Project Management Competency Development Framework*—Second Edition with the *PMP® Examination Specification*
- Aligned the *Project Management Competency Development Framework*—Second Edition with *PMBOK® Guide*—Third Edition
- Built upon the framework utilized in the first edition, in particular the Personal Competencies
- Provided examples of evidence required to demonstrate competence
- Strengthened the chapter on developing competence
- Included professional responsibility and ethics.

This standard has been restructured to realign the structure of the Performance Competencies. The Performance Competencies in the *PMCD Framework* are now viewed from a *process* perspective, making the model simpler and easier to use. The Personal Competency section now includes professional responsibility and ethics and has been revised to reflect project management Personal Competencies. The chapter on developing competence now includes a model for assessment, personal growth, and learning.

We would like to take this opportunity to recognize the many volunteers that participated in this project. Their sterling efforts provide the project management community with a standard that individual project managers and project management organizations are able to use to assess their current level of project management competence. They can then use this as an input to plan future development in a logical, structured way.

Chris Cartwright
Project Manager
PMCD Framework Project Team

Michael Yinger
Deputy Project Manager
PMCD Framework Project Team

Chapter 1

Introduction

The Project Manager Competency Development (PMCD) Framework—Second Edition provides a framework for the definition, assessment, and development of project manager competence. It defines the key dimensions of competence and identifies those competencies that are most likely to impact project manager performance. The degree of its impact on project success may vary, depending on factors such as project types and characteristics, or organizational context and maturity. The competencies identified by the *PMCD Framework*—Second Edition have a broad application. The potential differences in the importance of particular competencies, given certain organizational contexts or project types or characteristics, still need to be considered during the application of the *PMCD Framework*.

The *PMCD Framework* provides an overall view of the skills and behaviors one would need to develop competence as a project manager. The framework is comprised of four chapters:

● **Chapter 1 Introduction**—This chapter introduces the discussion and definition of project manager competence and provides an overview of the remaining chapters of the *PMCD Framework*.

● **Chapter 2 Performance Competencies**—This chapter provides a detailed description of the Performance Competencies applicable to project managers that are generally recognized as good practice when leading most projects, most of the time.

● **Chapter 3 Personal Competencies**—This chapter provides the detailed description of the Personal Competencies applicable to project managers when leading most projects, most of the time.

● **Chapter 4 Developing Competence as a Project Manager**—This chapter outlines a process for developing competence as a project manager.

Chapter 1 covers the following topics:

1.1 Purpose of the *PMCD Framework*
1.2 Target Audience
1.3 What is Project Manager Competence?
1.4 Alignment of the *PMCD Framework* with PMI Publications and Standards
1.5 Design of the *PMCD Framework*
1.6 Structure of the *PMCD Framework*
1.7 Application of the *PMCD Framework*

1.1 Purpose of the *PMCD Framework*

The *PMCD Framework* is sponsored by the Project Management Institute (PMI), and was first released in 2002. It was developed to provide both individuals and organizations with guidance on how to assess, plan, and manage the professional development of a project manager who:

- Has demonstrated the required project management knowledge, skills and experience,
- Has passed an accredited project management examination or certification (the Project Management Professional (PMP®) or an equivalent from a recognized institute), and
- Is able to provide evidence of Performance and Personal Competencies as identified in Chapters 2 and 3 of the *PMCD Framework.*

1.2 Target Audience

The *PMCD Framework* serves as a reference for individuals and organizations to establish and develop project management competence.

The target audience includes, but is not limited to the following:
- Project managers,
- Managers of project managers,
- Members of a Project Management Office,
- Managers responsible for establishing and developing project manager competence,
- Project sponsors,
- Educators teaching project management and other related subjects,
- Trainers developing project management educational programs,
- Consultants to the industry of project/program management,
- Human resource managers,
- Senior management, and
- Individuals interested in project management.

1.3 What is Project Manager Competence?

Competent project managers consistently apply their project management knowledge and personal behaviors to increase the likelihood of delivering projects that meet stakeholders' requirements. Project managers bring together their knowledge, skills, personal characteristics, and attitudes when focusing on delivering a project.

When applied to project management, *competence* is the demonstrated ability to perform activities within a project environment that lead to expected outcomes based on defined and accepted standards. (Crawford, L.H. 1997. A Global approach to project management. *Proceedings of the 1997 AIPM National Conference,* Gold Coast, 220–228.)

Project manager *competence* consists of three separate dimensions:
- *Project Manager Knowledge Competence*—What the project manager *knows* about the application of processes, tools, and techniques for project activities.
- *Project Manager Performance Competence*—How the project manager *applies* project management knowledge to meet the project requirements.
- *Project Manager Personal Competence*—How the project manager *behaves* when performing activities within the project environment; their attitudes, and core personality characteristics.

To be recognized as fully competent, a project manager would need to satisfy each of these three dimensions.

1.3.1 Competencies Addressed by the *PMCD Framework*

The three dimensions of competence—Knowledge, Performance, and Personal—are demonstrated in different ways:
- *Project Manager Knowledge Competence* can be demonstrated by passing an appropriately credentialed assessment, such as the *PMP® Examination,* or any equivalent international project manager accreditation. These knowledge competencies are detailed in the *PMP® Examination Specification* and are not defined in the *PMCD Framework.*

● *Project Manager Performance Competence* can be demonstrated by assessing the project-related actions and outcomes to be considered competent. These knowledge competencies are detailed in the PMP® Examination Specification. Project Manager Performance Competence can be demonstrated by assessing project-related outcomes. Appropriate outcomes are detailed in the PMP® Examination Specification.

● *Project Manager Personal Competence* can be demonstrated by assessing the project manager's behavior.

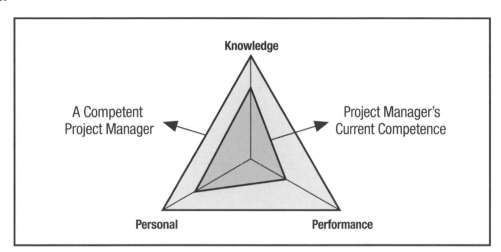

Figure 1-1. *PMCD Framework* dimensions of competence

Figure 1-1 illustrates the three dimensions for assessing project managers. As a result of the assessment, the project manager will better understand the skill development necessary to attain recognition as a competent project manager. The outer boundaries of the figure are a conceptual representation of a fully competent project manager. The shaded area may represent an individual project manager's current assessment of competence. The difference between the two areas represents the individual project manager's competence development needs.

The *PMCD Framework* provides the baseline to assess Performance and Personal Competencies.

1.3.2 Other Competence

The *PMCD Framework* is based upon the principles and processes of the *PMBOK® Guide*—Third Edition. It describes the generic competencies needed in most projects, most organizations, and most industries. In some industries there may be technical skills that are particularly relevant to that industry or covered by specific domain, regulatory, or legal requirements. For example, an organization primarily involved in conducting information technology projects may require that its project managers possess a specified level of information technology competence, as well as competence in project management. In other industries there may be regulations that are a constraint on the project manager. For example, an organization primarily involved in construction projects may require more knowledge of safety standards. A project manager needs to manage a project within the context of an industry and an organization.

The *PMCD Framework* does not address industry-specific competence. Individual project managers, or their organizations, may choose to supplement the *PMCD Framework* generic competencies with additional industry-specific competencies to meet their specific needs.

1.3.3 Complementing the *PMCD Framework*

The Performance and Personal Competencies in the *PMCD Framework* are comprised of units of competence. The units are comprised of elements of competence. The units and elements of competence in the *PMCD Framework* are intended to represent the project manager who would generally be accepted as competent. The *PMCD Framework* has been designed to apply to most projects most of the time. As depicted in Figure 1.2, the competencies described in Chapters 2 and 3 of the *PMCD Framework* should be used as a foundation for developing an assessment model.

The assessment model is then complemented by organizational and industry-specific performance requirements. The actual level of achievement of those competencies defines the project manager's competence. Figure 1-2, complementing the *PMCD Framework*, is a comprehensive representation of the competencies that a project manager would be expected to be assessed against.

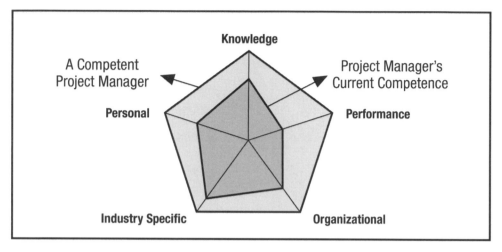

Figure 1-2. Complementing the *PMCD Framework*

1.4 Alignment *of the PMCD Framework with PMI Standards*

The *PMCD Framework* aligns with the general accepted practices promoted by PMI as reflected in corresponding standards and documents created or endorsed by PMI. *A Guide to the Project Management Body of Knowledge (PMBOK® Guide)*—Third Edition and the *PMP® Examination Specification* are core standards referenced by the *PMCD Framework*.

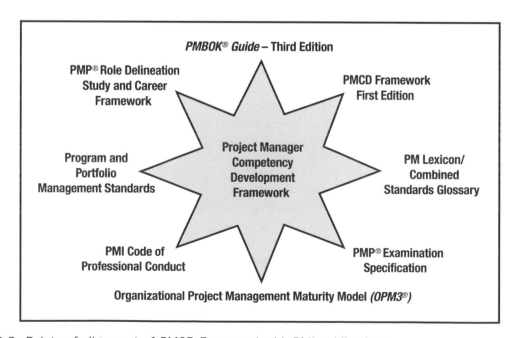

Figure 1-3. Points of alignment of *PMCD Framework* with PMI publications

The *PMCD Framework*—Second Edition is also aligned with other PMI publications and standards as illustrated in Figure 1-3. Details on the points of alignment are found in Table 1-1. To find all PMI publications, refer to www.pmi.org.

1.5 Design of the *PMCD Framework*

The *PMCD Framework* defines the dimensions of Performance and Personal Competence. As previously identified, Knowledge Competence is not detailed within the *PMCD Framework* as it is specifically addressed in the *PMP® Examination Specification*. The intent is to ensure that individuals, their organizations, and associated industry professional bodies apply an appropriate process for the assessment, development, and recognition of competence in project managers.

PMI Publications/Resources	Key Points of Alignment
A Guide to the Project Management Body of Knowledge (PMBOK® Guide) ^	The structure, vocabulary, and definitions of the current *PMBOK® Guide*.
PMCD Framework – First Edition	The structure and philosophy of the *PMCD Framework*.
PMI Combined Standards Glossary	The acronyms and terms identified in the PMI Combined Glossary.
PMP® Examination Specification	The required knowledge described therein. (The *PMCD Framework* refers to the PMP® Examination Specification for its definition of knowledge competencies).
Organizational Project Management Maturity Model (OPM3®)	The project manager competence module.
PMI Code of Ethics and Professional Conduct	The statement of the code of professional conduct under which a project manager operates.
The Standard for Program Management and The Standard for Portfolio Management	Project management is a core component of both standards.
Project Management Professional (PMP®) Role Delineation Study	The research indicating required knowledge, skills, and other data.
PMI's career framework	A web-based assessment and pathing tool which endorses project management competencies as the foundation for a project management career path.

^ All references to PMI publications and resources refer to the most current version available.

Table 1-1. Points of alignment of *PMCD Framework* with PMI resources

The *PMCD Framework* has been designed to:
- Cover the range of competencies the project manager needs to demonstrate.
- Apply generically to all project managers regardless of the nature, type, size, or complexity of projects in which they are engaged.

The generic nature of the *PMCD Framework* is necessary to ensure that:
- Project management competence in individuals is transferable across industries and organizations.
- Industries and organizations are able to utilize the *PMCD Framework* as a basis for the development of industry and organization-specific competence models.

Figure 1-4 shows the Performance and Personal Competencies as they align across the Knowledge Competence.

1.6 Structure of the *PMCD Framework*

The *PMCD Framework* breaks the desired competencies down into a simple structure. At the highest level are Units of Competence, which divide competencies into major segments, typically representing

Performance Competencies Chapter 2	Performance Competencies Chapter 3
Initiating a Project Planning a Project Executing a Project Monitoring and Controlling a Project Closing a Project	Communicating Leading Managing Cognitive Ability Effectiveness Professionalism
Knowledge Competence	

Figure 1-4 *PMCD Framework* graphical overview

a major function or activity. At the next tier are Elements of Competence, which are the basic building blocks of each unit. They describe, in output terms, actions or outcomes that are demonstrable or accessible. Each element is provided with a set of performance criteria which are the list of aspects of performance that are regarded as displaying competent performance of an Element of Competence. Each performance criteria includes a listing of the types of evidence or specific documented proof that the action within the performance criteria has been satisfied. In addition, Chapters 2 and 3 of the *PMCD Framework* use the following focus for their structure:

1.6.1 Units of Competence:
- *Chapter 2*—Specific Performance Domains from the PMP examination. Specification, except Professional Responsibility which is covered in Chapter 3.
- *Chapter 3*—Personal Competencies, specific to project managers.

1.6.2 Elements of Competence:
- Each Unit of Competence consists of a number of elements that reflect the activities in which project managers are expected to be competent.
- In Chapter 2, elements are project outcomes.
- In Chapter 3, elements are project manager behaviors.

1.6.3 Performance Criteria:
- Each element is described by performance criteria that specify the actions required to demonstrate competent performance.

1.6.4 Types of Evidence:
- Performance criteria are achieved by producing specific proof that the action has been completed.
- These form the basis upon which competence can be assessed.
  Figure 1-5 depicts the structure used by Chapters 2 and 3 of the *PMCD Framework*.

1.7 Application of the *PMCD Framework*

The *PMCD Framework* provides important guidance to practitioners, employers, and advisors when setting up a competency framework in the workplace. It is important to become comfortable with the contents of the *PMCD Framework* and what it indicates with regard to project manager compe-

©2007 Project Management Institute, Four Campus Boulevard, Newtown Square, PA 19073-3299 USA

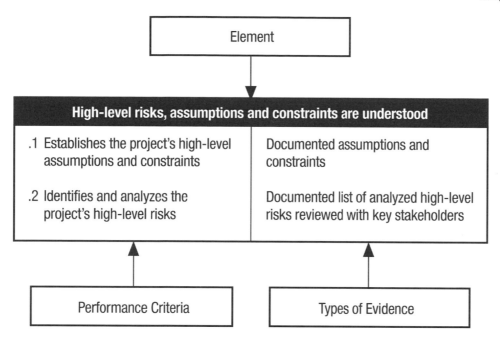

Note: This is an example of part of a Performance Competence Element.

Figure 1-5 Structure of Competence Units with the *PMCD Framework*

tence. The *PMCD Framework* provides a summary of the competencies that support project manager performance.

The *PMCD Framework* defines project manager competence by identifying performance criteria relative to specific elements and units of competence. Understanding the individual project manager's current capability is essential to establishing a competence baseline. Measuring individual performance against a competence baseline will identify the project manager's strengths and development needs. The dimension of Personal Competence looks at the project manager's behavior relative to overall competence in managing projects. The goal is to meet or exceed the baseline competence defined by the *PMCD Framework*.

• For **employers,** the *PMCD Framework* provides a multidimensional taxonomy of the actions and behaviors typically required by project managers in order to fulfill their role within the organization. The *PMCD Framework* can be used to identify the existing competence of project managers, as well as any gaps that should be addressed. There may be project type, industry, or technology-specific requirements that are needed to complement the *PMCD Framework*. The *PMCD Framework* can be used to determine the competence of individuals who manage projects within the organization.

• For **practicing project managers**, the *PMCD Framework* provides assistance in determining their own level of competence and areas where further development is required.

• For **advisors** to an organization, the *PMCD Framework* provides a powerful tool to help scan and analyze the existing actions and outcomes within the organization to discover any gaps that may need to be addressed.

• For **individuals** who are considering moving into project management, the *PMCD Framework* provides a guide to the competencies they will be expected to develop.

The *PMCD Framework* provides an assessment process which allows project managers (or managers of project managers) to identify their strengths and development needs within the competence framework. It assists in the identification of options for improvement, and how to develop and implement a competence development plan.

Chapter 2

Performance Competencies

Performance Competence is what the project manager is able to do or accomplish by applying their project management knowledge.

Individuals will demonstrate their Performance Competence by applying their knowledge and skills to a project and delivering the planned outcomes. Each individual skill that reflects project management good practice needs to be assessed. To assess Performance Competence, endorsed standards or baselines are required for each skill against which:

● Individuals are able to measure and plan their progress towards competence. Organizations are able to design performance measurement instruments, design job specifications, employment specifications. and individual development programs.

● Performance Competencies in the *PMCD Framework*—Second Edition are aligned with five of the six Performance Domains from the PMP Examination Specification. The sixth domain, Professional Responsibility, is included in Chapter 3 on Personal Competencies.

● Units cover the skills that need to be addressed in order to demonstrate specific competencies.

● Performance Competence can be measured by assessing individuals against each Unit of Competence and element using the performance criteria and types of evidence specified in this chapter.

The Performance Criteria given in this document need to be tailored to the individual organization in accordance with the organizational project management processes and the project management policies, in accordance with their applicability.

This chapter covers the following topics

2.1 Purpose of Performance Competencies
2.2 Structure of Performance Competencies
2.3 Performance Criteria and Types of Evidence
2.4 Units of Performance Competence

2.1 Purpose of the Performance Competencies

Performance Competence puts into practice the knowledge and skills that a project manager possesses. It is generally accepted that there is a causal link between project manager competence and project success. Performance Competence is a key component of overall project manager competence. The Performance Competencies in this chapter provide the framework, structure, and baselines against which an individual may be measured. Assessing performance competence of project managers and closing any gaps may help individuals and their organizations to maximize project manager competence. The five Units of Performance Competence described in this chapter provide one important dimension of the framework for that assessment.

2.2 Structure of the Performance Competencies

The *PMCD Framework*—Second Edition uses the *PMBOK® Guide*—3rd Edition and the *PMP® Examination Specification* to define the structure of the units of Performance Competence. The Professional Responsibility domain of the PMP Examination Specification is covered under Personal Competencies (Chapter 3). The five units resulting from the Performance Domains of the Examination Specification as shown in Figure 2-1 are:

- *Initiating a Project*—Performing the work to authorize and define the preliminary scope of a new project.
- *Planning a Project*—Performing the work to define and mature the project scope, develop the project management plan, and identify and schedule the project activities.
- *Executing a Project*—Performing the work defined in the project management plan to accomplish the project objectives under the project scope statement.
- *Monitoring and Controlling a Project*—Performing the work to compare actual performance with planned performance, analyze variances, assess trends to effect process improvements, evaluate possible alternatives, and implement appropriate corrective action as needed.
- *Closing a Project*—Performing the work to formally terminate a project and transfer the completed product to operations or to close a cancelled project.

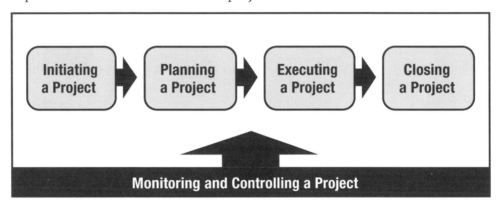

Figure 2-1. The Five Units of Performance Competence

As illustrated in Figure 2-2, each unit of competence is composed of a number of elements required for a competent project manager. Each element is described as an *outcome* to be achieved.

2.3 Performance Criteria and Types of Evidence

Each element is further defined in the terms of ***performance criteria,*** which specify what the individual needs to do to demonstrate competent performance in each element (see Figure 2-3). Individual performance criteria can be assessed using the ***types of evidence*** defined in the tables of this chapter. When the individual performs the activities described in the performance criteria there must be an outcome that provides some type of evidence. This may include deliverables, documents, and feedback from a stakeholder or some other tangible or intangible result. Assessment requires that some form of evidence be reviewed to determine the degree of compliance with the performance criteria. The *PMCD Framework* provides examples of such evidence for each criterion. Assessors should note that the *PMCD Framework* provides these examples as general guidance and to provide context for an assessment plan. The examples are not standards nor expected outcomes. Project outcomes will reflect cultures, organizations and industries. As such, assessors can expect variance in the outcomes found among projects.

In the *PMCD Framework,* the term "documented" means tangible evidence. In this context "documented" is inclusive of data, any form of media, formal or informal correspondence, objects, and outputs.

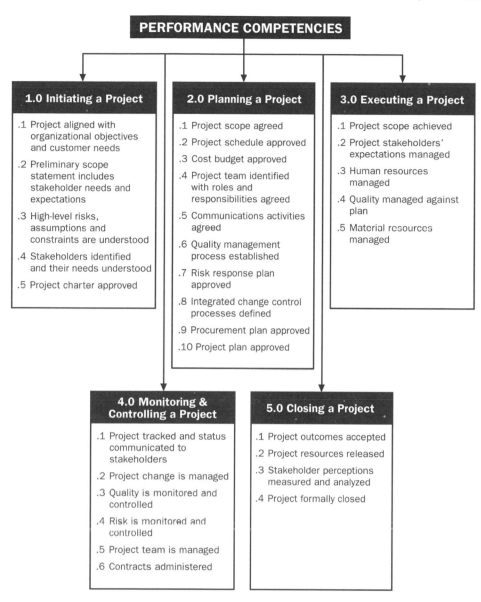

PERFORMANCE COMPETENCIES

1.0 Initiating a Project

.1 Project aligned with organizational objectives and customer needs

.2 Preliminary scope statement includes stakeholder needs and expectations

.3 High-level risks, assumptions and constraints are understood

.4 Stakeholders identified and their needs understood

.5 Project charter approved

2.0 Planning a Project

.1 Project scope agreed

.2 Project schedule approved

.3 Cost budget approved

.4 Project team identified with roles and responsibilities agreed

.5 Communications activities agreed

.6 Quality management process established

.7 Risk response plan approved

.8 Integrated change control processes defined

.9 Procurement plan approved

.10 Project plan approved

3.0 Executing a Project

.1 Project scope achieved

.2 Project stakeholders' expectations managed

.3 Human resources managed

.4 Quality managed against plan

.5 Material resources managed

4.0 Monitoring & Controlling a Project

.1 Project tracked and status communicated to stakeholders

.2 Project change is managed

.3 Quality is monitored and controlled

.4 Risk is monitored and controlled

.5 Project team is managed

.6 Contracts administered

5.0 Closing a Project

.1 Project outcomes accepted

.2 Project resources released

.3 Stakeholder perceptions measured and analyzed

.4 Project formally closed

Figure 2-2. Units and Elements of Performance Competence

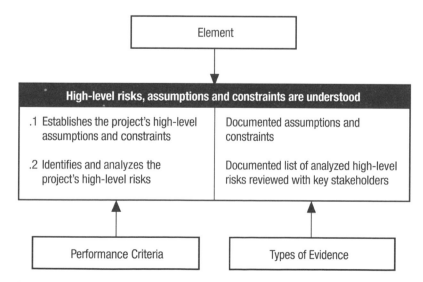

Element

High-level risks, assumptions and constraints are understood

.1 Establishes the project's high-level assumptions and constraints	Documented assumptions and constraints
.2 Identifies and analyzes the project's high-level risks	Documented list of analyzed high-level risks reviewed with key stakeholders

Performance Criteria

Types of Evidence

Figure 2-3. Example of an Element, Performance Criteria and Types of Evidence

2.4 Units Of Performance Competence

The purpose of *PMCD Framework* is to highlight the project management competencies required of project managers, in most projects, most of the time. The Performance Competence units identified in Chapter 1 are described in the following sections.

1.0 Unit of Competence: Initiating a Project	
Performing the work to authorize a new project and define its scope.	
Element 1.1 Project aligned with organizational objectives and customer needs	
Performance Criteria	**Types of Evidence**
.1 Understands the project alignment	Description of the project alignment
.2 Achieves agreement on project alignment with project sponsor	Documented agreement with sponsor
.3 Establishes key stakeholders' needs and expectations	Documented stakeholders' needs for a project
.4 Determines product or service characteristics	Documented high-level stakeholder requirements for products and services linked to a project plan used in delivering a project
Element 1.2 Preliminary scope statement reflects stakeholder needs and expectations	
Performance Criteria	**Types of Evidence**
.1 Selects and uses a suitable project management methodology or process	Examples of methods used in previous projects and an explanation of why it was chosen
.2 Understands the preliminary scope of the project	Preliminary scope statement or equivalent
.3 Frames high-level project scope ensuring alignment with organization and customer needs and expectations	Documented stakeholders' needs for a project
Element 1.3 High-level risks, assumptions and constraints are understood	
Performance Criteria	**Types of Evidence**
.1 Establishes the project's high-level assumptions and constraints	Documented assumptions and constraints
.2 Identifies, qualifies and quantifies the project's high-level risks	Risk register containing identified, qualified and quantified high-level risks

Table 2-1. Performance Competence—Initiating a Project *(continued)*

Element 1.4 Stakeholders identified and their needs are understood	
Performance Criteria	**Types of Evidence**
.1 Identifies project stakeholders	Documented list of stakeholders
.2 Conducts stakeholder analysis to gain buy-in and identify needs for the project	Documented description of stakeholder needs and objectives Documented stakeholders position and influence
.3 Identifies high-level communication requirements	Documented feedback from stakeholders acknowledging their needs were understood Communications management plan Documented high-level communication strategy
Element 1.5 Project charter approved	
Performance Criteria	**Types of Evidence**
.1 Develops a high-level project strategy	Documented high-level project strategy
.2 Establishes the project's key milestones and deliverables	Documented milestones and deliverables
.3 Develops summary budget	Documented order of magnitude effort estimate
.4 Supports the project charter preparation	Documented resource requirements Documented summary budget Draft project charter documents
.5 Uses governance process to obtain sponsor approval and commitment	Approved project charter, with governance documentation e.g. business cases, stage gate meeting minutes

Table 2-1. Performance Competence—Initiating a Project *(concluded)*

2.0 Unit of Competence: Planning a Project	
Performing the work to define and mature the project scope, develop the project management plan, and identify and schedule the project activities.	

Element 2.1 Project scope agreed	
Performance Criteria	**Types of Evidence**
.1 Defines project deliverables using a work breakdown structure (WBS)	WBS List of project alternatives
.2 Obtains agreement for the scope defined by the WBS	Documented agreement from project stakeholders
.3 Implements scope management	Feedback from stakeholders Scope management plan

Element 2.2 Project schedule approved	
Performance Criteria	**Types of Evidence**
.1 Defines activities and dependencies to deliver approved scope	Project schedule network diagrams WBS Dictionary
.2 Estimates time for completion of each activity	Documentation of the process used to determine schedule task durations
.3 Identifies internal and external dependencies	Project schedule with schedule model data
.4 Schedules the project activities against the resource commitments	Project schedule with schedule model data
.5 Obtains approval for the project schedule	Documented sponsor approval of project schedule
.6 Communicates project schedule with stakeholders	Documented feedback from stakeholders Documented agreement from project stakeholders

Element 2.3 Cost budget approved	
Performance Criteria	**Types of Evidence**
.1 Estimates costs for each activity	Examples of activity based costing Approved budget with supporting detail
.2 Estimates all other project costs	Approved budget with supporting detail
.3 Develops the project budget	Approved budget with supporting detail
.4 Develops cost management plan	Cost management plan
.5 Gains approval for the planned project budget	Documented sponsor approval of project budget
.6 Communicates planned budget to stakeholders	Documented feedback from stakeholders

Table 2-2. Performance Competence—Planning a Project *(continued)*

Element 2.4 Project team identified with roles and responsibilities agreed	
Performance Criteria	**Types of Evidence**
.1 Identifies specific resources	Staff management plan with roles and responsibilities
.2 Defines roles and responsibilities	Documented team members and stakeholders roles and responsibilities Documented team protocols
.3 Reaches agreement with the organization for access to suitable resources	Documented formal agreements for resources
.4 Plans resource ramp up and team building	Documented activities for team development and resource ramp up Documented team rules
Element 2.5 Communication activities agreed	
Performance Criteria	**Types of Evidence**
.1 Builds a project communication plan	Communication management plan
.2 Selects suitable tools and methods to communicate with identified stakeholders	Templates to support plan e.g. status report, issue log, lessons learned or other organizational process assets
.3 Schedules activities to address the communication plan	Documented feedback from stakeholders
Element 2.6 Quality Management process established	
Performance Criteria	**Types of Evidence**
.1 Establishes quality standards to be used within the project that aligns with organizational quality policy	Documentation of the quality standards used
.2 Defines processes to be used to deliver the project deliverables	Project quality process documentation
.3 Establishes project quality metrics for deliverables, processes and project management performance	Documentation of project quality metrics
.4 Develops a project quality management plan	Approved project quality management plan including quality baseline

Table 2-2. Performance Competence—Planning a Project *(continued)*

Element 2.7 Risk response plan approved	
Performance Criteria	**Types of Evidence**
.1 Develops project risk management plan	Approved risk management plan for project
.2 Identifies and quantifies major risks	Documented results of risk analysis Risk register
.3 Leads/delegates the effort to find response strategies for each identified risk	Risk response plan including nominated risk owners and contingency costs
.4 Estimates risk contingency costs	Risk response plan including nominated risk owners and contingency costs
.5 Documents risk response plan	Risk response plan including nominated risk owners and contingency costs
.6 Assigns risks responsibility	List of risk owners Risk register
.7 Gains agreement from key stakeholders for the project risk response plan	Documented feedback from key stakeholders

Element 2.8 Integrated change control processes defined	
Performance Criteria	**Types of Evidence**
.1 Leads/delegates the effort to establish a change control process	Documented integrated change control process
.2 Involves stakeholders in generating change control plan	Documentation of stakeholder involvement in formulating change control plan
.3 Ensures the use of a change control processes and procedures	Minutes of Change Control Board (CCB) meetings Change control documentation
.4 Communicates with key stakeholders on change control process	Documented feedback from key stakeholders

Table 2-2. Performance Competence—Planning a Project *(continued)*

Element 2.9 Procurement plan approved	
Performance Criteria	**Types of Evidence**
.1 Analyzes material requirements	Project procurement management plan Bills of materials
.2 Plans purchases and acquisitions	Purchase requests and orders
.3 Plans external labor procurement	Documentation to support external labor procurement Resource contracts
.4 Plans contract administration	Procurement management plan
.5 Obtains plan approval	Sponsor approval of procurement management plan
Element 2.10 Project plan approved	
Performance Criteria	**Types of Evidence**
.1 Reviews organizational process assets	Documented review and/or use of organizational process assets
.2 Reviews enterprise environmental factors	Documented review and/or use of enterprise environmental factors
.3 Integrates the planning activities into a complete project management plan	Documentation showing how elements of the project management plan integrates
.4 Seeks approval by key stakeholders	Project management plan approved by key stakeholders
.5 Establishes project baselines	Documented project baselines
.6 Communicates approved plan to key stakeholders	Documented feedback from stakeholders
.7 Conducts kick-off meeting	Agenda/minutes of kick-off meeting

Table 2-2. Performance Competence—Planning a Project *(concluded)*

3.0 Unit of Competence: Executing a Project	
Performing the work in the project management plan to accomplish the project objectives under the project scope statement.	

Element 3.1 Project scope achieved	
Performance Criteria	**Types of Evidence**
.1 Verifies task completion as defined in the project plan	Documented feedback from key stakeholders Documented project tracking actions and status Status/milestone reports Formal acceptance documentation confirming tasks completed successfully Project cost reports showing planned versus actual completion and resource utilization
.2 Closes identified performance gaps	Documentation of corrective and preventive action
.3 Executes risk management plan	Documentation of corrective and preventive action
.4 Manages phase transitions	Governance meetings, actions, minutes Feedback from sponsor Formal approvals

Element 3.2 Project stakeholders' expectations managed	
Performance Criteria	**Types of Evidence**
.1 Reviews stakeholder expectations throughout the project to ensure they are being met within the project scope	Documentation of updates to stakeholder analysis Documentation of actions taken to manage stakeholders expectations
.2 Interacts with stakeholders to ensure support for the project	Minutes of all stakeholder meetings Documentation of actions taken to manage stakeholders expectations Documented feedback from stakeholders

Element 3.3 Human resources managed	
Performance Criteria	**Types of Evidence**
.1 Acquires human resources per staff management plan	Staffing lists Labor contracts Statements of work (SOW) for procured labor
.2 Builds project team	Project organization chart Documented ways of working
.3 Develops project team members	Competence gap analysis Development plan for team members

Table 2-3. Performance Competence—Executing a Project *(continued)*

Element 3.4 Quality managed against plan	
Performance Criteria	**Types of Evidence**
.1 Executes quality assurance activities	Documented acceptance of project deliverables by key stakeholders Documented change requests
.2 Ensures compliance with quality standards and processes	Quality audits Documented process improvement recommendations Documented updates to planning documents based on variance from plan
Element 3.5 Material resources managed	
Performance Criteria	**Types of Evidence**
.1 Requests seller information	List of selected sellers Seller responses
.2 Selects suitable sellers	Contracts, SOWs Purchase orders
.3 Executes procurement tasks against schedule commitment	Documented availability of material resources
.4 Acquires internally supplied resources	Documented availability of material resources

Table 2-3. Performance Competence—Executing a Project *(concluded)*

4.0 Unit of Competence: Monitoring and Controlling a Project	
Performing the work to compare actual performance with planned performance, to analyze variances, to assess trends to effect process improvements, to evaluate possible alternatives, and to implement appropriate corrective action as needed.	
Element 4.1 Project tracked and status communicated to stakeholders	
Performance Criteria	**Types of Evidence**
.1 Executes the process for capturing project information	Project performance reports
.2 Communicates status to stakeholders	Minutes of regular meeting or status reports Documented feedback from stakeholders Performance measurements
.3 Ensures action plans are put in place to address any variations to plan	Documented corrective and preventive action plan taken to recover variations
Element 4.2 Project change is managed	
Performance Criteria	**Types of Evidence**
.1 Identifies changes to baseline project plans	Written change requests submitted for action, authorized by the designated approvers Updates to project plan as a result of approved changes.
.2 Identifies the impact of the changes to the project plan	Documented results of the analysis of the changes
.3 Follows the change management process to manage and record changes	Records of approved and implemented changes
.4 Communicates changes to project stakeholders	Documented communications to stakeholders
.5 Execute configuration management process	Documented feedback from stakeholders about configuration management and control practices
Element 4.3 Quality is monitored and controlled	
Performance Criteria	**Types of Evidence**
.1 Records acceptance of completed deliverables	Records of completed and signed-off deliverables
.2 Collects project and product metrics	Project and product metric reports
.3 Monitors deviation from project baselines	Quality defects reports
.4 Recommends corrective and preventive actions	Documentation of corrective and preventive actions
.5 Facilitates audits	Audit reports Documented suggestions for improvement

Table 2-4. Performance Competence—Monitoring and Controlling a Project *(continued)*

Element 4.4 Risk is monitored and controlled	
Performance Criteria	**Types of Evidence**
.1 Updates risk response plan	Updated risk register Documentation of results of risk response plan
.2 Recognizes when unknown risks occur	Documentation of previously unknown risks that occur Updated risk register
.3 Establishes workarounds for previously unknown risks	Documentation of workarounds for previously unknown risks Updated risk response plan
.4 Recognizes new risk	Updated risk register
.5 Reviews risk response strategies	Documented results of risk mitigation reviews
.6 Facilitates audits	Audit reports Documented suggestions for improvement
Element 4.5 Project team managed	
Performance Criteria	**Types of Evidence**
.1 Holds regular team meetings.	Minutes of team meetings
.2 Conducts team building activities	Documented results of team building activities
.3 Monitors team satisfaction	Results of team satisfaction survey
.4 Provides feedback on team and individual member performance	Documented feedback given on a team member Documentation of team feedback
Element 4.6 Contracts administered	
Performance Criteria	**Types of Evidence**
.1 Ensures seller contracts are effectively managed	Feedback from sellers
.2 Collects seller performance metrics	Seller performance metrics reports
.3 Ensures sellers are part of the project team culture	Documentation of seller interaction and integration with the team Seller satisfaction surveys
.4 Facilitates audits	Audit reports Documented suggestions for improvement

Table 2-4. Performance Competence—Monitoring and Controlling a Project *(concluded)*

5.0 Unit of Competence: Closing a Project	
Performing the work to formally terminate a project and transfer the completed product to operations or to close a cancelled project.	
Element 5.1 Project outcomes accepted	
Performance Criteria	**Types of Evidence**
.1 Obtains final acceptance	Documented approval of project outcome
.2 Meets all contractual requirements where required	Documentation of finished and unfinished deliverables Documented acceptance that terms of the contract have been met
.3 Transitions all deliverables to operations	Documented acceptance by operations
Element 5.2 Project resources released	
Performance Criteria	**Types of Evidence**
.1 Executes the organizational processes for releasing project resources	Example of a timetable for project team member release schedule from a project as it was closed
.2 Provides performance feedback to project team members	Documented staff performance feedback
.3 Provides feedback to the organization regarding team members' performance	Performance evaluation reviewed with functional managers and stored.
Element 5.3 Stakeholder perceptions measured and analyzed	
Performance Criteria	**Types of Evidence**
.1 Surveys project stakeholders	Documented feedback from stakeholders
.2 Analyzes results of feedback	Documented analysis
Element 5.4 Project formally closed	
Performance Criteria	**Types of Evidence**
.1 Executes closure activities for the project	Signed acknowledgement of project products or services delivered and documentation of closing activities
.2 Closes all financial activities associated with project	Documented feedback from finance department on project closure
.3 Notifies stakeholders formally of project closure	Document communicating project closure stored in project file
.4 Closes all project contracts	Contracts closed as required
.5 Documents and publishes project learning	Documentation of lessons learned
.6 Updates organizational process assets	Archived project documents Documented changes to organizational process assets

Table 2-5. Performance Competence—Closing a Project *(concluded)*

Chapter 3

Personal Competencies

Personal Competencies are those behaviors, attitudes, and core personality characteristics that contribute to a person's ability to manage projects.

The Personal Competencies presented in this chapter combine with the knowledge competencies described in the *PMBOK Guide*—Third Edition, and with the Performance Competencies described in Chapter 2 of this document. As described in Chapter 1, there are certain overlaps between Knowledge, Performance and Personal Competencies. For example, this chapter may describe the behavior supporting specific actions of performance competence. Taken together, the three dimensions of competence are required by a project manager to deliver most projects most of the time.

This chapter covers the following topics

3.1 **Purpose of Personal Competencies**
3.2 **Structure of Personal Competencies**
3.3 **Personal Criteria and Types of Evidence**
3.4 **Units of Personal Competence**

3.1 Purpose of Personal Competencies

Project management is a people-oriented profession. It is important for a project manager to possess skills that enable an effective interaction with others. Personal Competencies describe such skills.

Improvements in Personal Competence enhance a project manager's ability to use Knowledge and Performance Competence effectively on projects. The treatment of Personal Competencies as given in this chapter provides a basis for assessing and developing the ability of individuals with regard to the personal competence elements described in this chapter.

3.2 Structure of Personal Competencies

Personal Competencies are grouped into the following six (6) units:
• **Communicating**—Effectively exchanges accurate, appropriate, and relevant information with stakeholders using suitable methods.
• **Leading**—Guides, inspires, and motivates team members and other project stakeholders to manage and overcome issues to effectively achieve project objectives.
• **Managing**—Effectively administers the project through deployment and use of human, financial, material, intellectual, and intangible resources.

- **Cognitive Ability**—Applies an appropriate depth of perception, discernment, and judgment to effectively direct a project in a changing and evolving environment.
- **Effectiveness**—Produces desired results by using appropriate resources, tools, and techniques in all project management activities.
- **Professionalism**—Conforms to an ethical behavior governed by responsibility, respect, fairness, and honesty in the practice of project management

There are elements within each of the Personal Competencies that overlap or are very similar to the other competencies. In addition there are individual capabilities that will be outside of a project manager's Personal Competencies as defined in this document. Figure 3-1 shows this relationship.

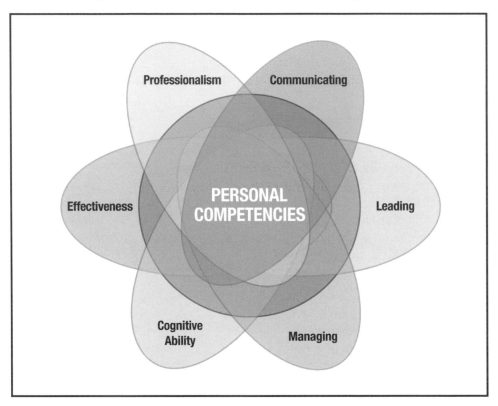

Figure 3-1. Personal Competencies

3.3 Performance Criteria and Types of Evidence

Each unit is composed of several Competence Elements considered necessary for an individual to have Personal Competence. Performance criteria describe the behaviors that show each competence element. While it is generally difficult to show objective proof of human behavior, the types of evidence provide examples that could reflect the achievement of a certain performance criteria.

Figure 3-2 describes the typical structure of a Competence Element.

Some examples of evidence are project documents, while others are documented observations of a person's behavior by stakeholders or team members. There are instances where some of the evidence may apply to more than one performance criteria; the duplication of evidence is deliberate, given that the behavior can vary from one unit to another, while the type of evidence used to demonstrate may be the same. The type of evidence should guide the assessor, but the evidence outlined should not be seen as prescriptive, but rather as a typical example.

Figure 3-3 summarizes all the units of Personal Competencies in this chapter along with the supporting elements within each unit.

©2007 Project Management Institute, Four Campus Boulevard, Newtown Square, PA 19073-3299 USA

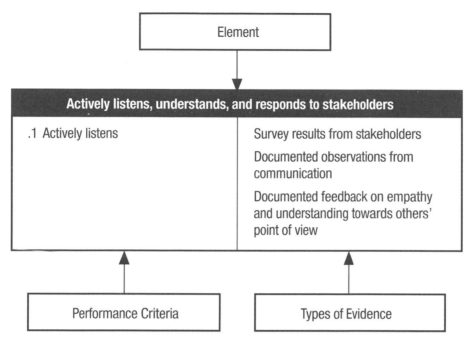

Figure 3-2. Structure of Competence Elements

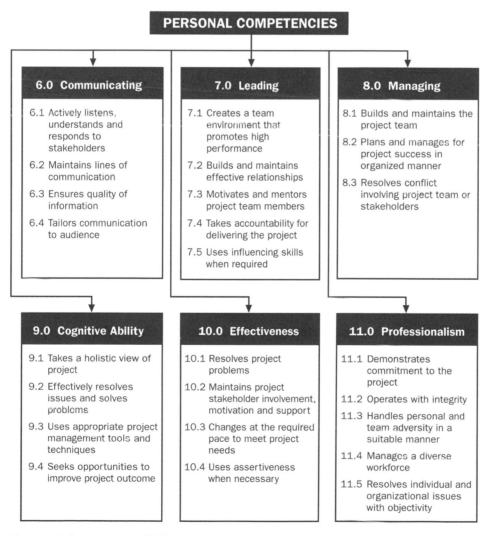

Figure 3-3. Personal Competence Units

3.4 Units of Personal Competence

The purpose of *PMCD Framework* is to highlight the project management competencies required of project managers, in most projects, most of the time. The Personal Competence units identified in Chapter 1 are described in the following sections.

6.0 Unit of Competence: Communicating	
Effectively exchanges accurate, appropriate and relevant information with stakeholders using suitable methods.	
Element 6.1 Actively listens, understands, and responds to stakeholders	
Performance Criteria	**Types of Evidence**
.1 Actively listens	Survey results from stakeholders Documented observations from communication Documented feedback on empathy and understanding towards others point of view
.2 Understands explicit and implicit content of communication	Documented observations from communication Documented confirmation that messages were received and understood
.3 Responds to and acts upon expectations, concerns and issues	Documented responses to issues important to others (i.e. issues log) Change requests Survey results from stakeholders
Element 6.2 Maintains lines of communication	
Performance Criteria	**Types of Evidence**
.1 Engages stakeholders proactively	Documented confirmation that stakeholders needs have been met proactively
.2 Disseminates information effectively	Documentation that the communication was effective through conversation, survey, notes, presentations or observation Documentation of relevant and timely communication shared with appropriate stakeholders
.3 Maintains formal and informal communication	Minutes from planned and unplanned meetings, brainstorming sessions, etc. Correspondence Notes and follow-ups from discussions Documented feedback on availability to stakeholders

Table 3-1. Personal Competence—Closing a Project *(continued)*

Element 6.3 Ensures quality of information	
Performance Criteria	**Types of Evidence**
.1 Uses appropriate information sources	Documentation of sources and analysis Documented feedback on the sources
.2 Provides accurate and factual information	Documents showing that factual information is provided Documented feedback on the accuracy of the information
.3 Seeks validation of information	Documentation of input from subject matter experts (e.g. interest groups, professional bodies etc.) Meeting minutes
Element 6.4 Tailors communication to audience	
Performance Criteria	**Types of Evidence**
.1 Provides relevant information	Documented feedback from recipient confirming information relevance Demonstrated strong presentation skills
.2 Uses suitable communication method for the audience	Preferred communication methods identified in stakeholders' analysis Notes from meetings demonstrating suitability of method selection Feedback from stakeholders regarding suitability of method selection
.3 Aligns communication with environment or setting	Documented feedback on: • Sensitivity to others' specific communication needs and context • Appropriate use of formal, informal verbal, nonverbal, and para-lingual components • Minutes from team meetings or presentations • Examples of various choices of location, time, participants, and privacy settings

Table 3-1. Personal Competence—Closing a Project *(concluded)*

7.0 Unit of Competence: Leading
Guides, inspires and motivates team members and other project stakeholders to manage and overcome issues to effectively achieve project objectives.

Element 7.1 Creates a team environment that promotes high performance	
Performance Criteria	**Types of Evidence**
.1 Expresses positive expectations of team	Documented feedback from team on: • Recognizing abilities of team members • Supporting decision making • Setting positive expectations
.2 Promotes team learning and advocates professional and personal development	Individual development plans Funding for development Documented feedback from project team Documentation of new skills gained by the team members
.3 Encourages teamwork consistently	Examples of creative actions taken to encourage teamwork, respect for different opinions and personalities Documented feedback on acknowledgement of unique skills and abilities Identified responsibilities of team leaders in giving clear, consistent goals
.4 Demands and models high performance	Documented standards for individual performance and quality Documented results of project manager performing to standards Documented feedback that the project manager is acting as a role model Examples of holding project members accountable for their commitments

Element 7.2 Builds and maintains effective relationships	
Performance Criteria	**Types of Evidence**
.1 Confines relationships to work-related matters appropriate to the project and local culture	Documented feedback from project team and stakeholders on project manger maintaining formal working relationship with stakeholders Documented guidelines for formal and informal discussion
.2 Builds trust and confidence with stakeholders	Examples of: • Acting with integrity in all situations • Keeping commitments • Providing consistent messages in all situations • Supporting team members when confronted with unjustified criticism • Maintaining composure • Demonstrating fair treatment of partners and sellers
.3 Creates an environment that encourages openness, respect and consideration of stakeholders	Feedback from stakeholders on openness of issues analysis and resolution Open door policy (is approachable at all times for project-related matters) Examples of sensitivity and genuine interest in feelings and values of others Documented evidence of fair and fact-based decisions

Table 3-2. Personal Competence—Leading *(continued)*

Element 7.3 Motivates and mentors project team members	
Performance Criteria	**Types of Evidence**
.1 Establishes and communicates to the team the project vision, mission statement, and strategic value	Examples of presentations with clear focus on vision, mission, and strategic value Documented feedback from team regarding awareness of strategic value of the project Examples of rallying support behind the strategy and sharing the strategy with team members
.2 Rewards performance according to organization guidelines	Documented rewards and recognition records Examples of plans for success of team members Examples of celebrating individual accomplishments on a frequent basis; assures credit is given to the individual
.3 Establishes mentoring relationships for team members' development	Examples of mentoring relationships Examples of being sought out as a mentor for others Documented feedback on mentoring activities Examples of progress on individual development plan
Element 7.4 Takes accountability for delivering the project	
Performance Criteria	**Types of Evidence**
.1 Demonstrates ownership of, accountability for, and commitment to the project	Examples of active involvement with all stakeholders and project team members Examples of quickly addressing possible project hindrances, delays, or risks Reports or meeting notes where the project manager takes responsibility for project mishaps Examples of taking ownership for adverse project outcomes
.2 Aligns personal activities and priorities toward increasing likelihood of achieving project goals	Documented priority planning Lists of prioritized action items Examples of active event management
.3 Supports and promotes team's actions and decisions	Documented feedback from project team members that project manager acts assertively on their behalf Meeting notes reflecting project manager's support for team's actions and decisions Keeps abreast of project team activities and maintains accountability for delivery of work Takes a stand in front of higher authorities to support team's project actions as if they were their own
Element 7.5 Uses influencing skills when required	
Performance Criteria	**Types of Evidence**
.1 Applies appropriate influencing technique to each stakeholder	Examples of different styles on different occasions Document describing alternative approaches used to influence Examples of strong facilitation and negotiation skills Examples of the ability to educate
.2 Uses experts or third parties to persuade others	Examples of using positional power of others to influence Examples of using a third party's knowledge power to influence Examples of networking and gathering support for the project while not manipulating for personal gain

Table 3-2. Personal Competence—Leading *(concluded)*

8.0 Unit of Competence: Managing	
Effectively administers the project through appropriate deployment and use of human, financial, material, intellectual, and intangible resources.	
Element 8.1 Builds and maintains the project team	
Performance Criteria	**Types of Evidence**
.1 Ensures expectations and responsibilities are clear to team members and they understand their importance to the project	Documented feedback from project team on clarity of roles and responsibilities Team correspondence Documented project directives, tasks, and assignments Published Resource Assignment Matrix (RAM) Examples of active participation of each member to team activities
.2 Maintains a positive attitude and effective relationships among team members	Examples of effective conflict resolution Documented feedback from team members demonstrating: • Respect for others by appealing to reason in project context • Genuinely valuing input and expertise of others on the team • Willingness to learn from others Examples of team events to facilitate bonding and rapport within the team Celebration of team work and achievements
.3 Identifies, evaluates, and selects internal and external talent	Project resource requirements documentation Inventories of suitable team members identified from internal talent pool Predefined selection criteria applied to resources acquisition
.4 Promotes healthy work—life balance	Documented feedback from project team members Meeting notes documenting balance issues Documented plan of action to achieve balance Examples of actions taken to improve job efficiency and productivity

Table 3-3. Personal Competence—Managing (*continued*)

Element 8.2 Plans and manages for project success in an organized manner	
Performance Criteria	**Types of Evidence**
.1 Works with others to clearly identify project scope, roles, expectations, and tasks specifications	Documented feedback on level of involvement of others in the planning process
.2 Applies organization or industry standards and generally accepted practices to the project	Examples and feedback from project team, stakeholders and subject matter experts on following industry generally accepted practices Membership in Project Management Institute (PMI), Specific Interest Groups (SIGs), workshops, conferences, or organizations Proposed measures and improvements intended to achieve or exceed industry generally accepted practices Project plan that incorporates industry standards
.3 Tailors generally accepted practices for successful completion of the project	Documented change of generally accepted practices Approved changes to project management procedures to accommodate generally accepted practices
.4 Organizes project information, emphasizing appropriate levels of detail	Examples of standard methodologies used in project Meeting minutes Project status reports or updates Repository for project artifacts Examples of knowledge management
.5 Insists on compliance with processes, procedures, and policies	Monitored compliance of processes, procedures, and policies Examples of enforcing policies and procedures Documented use of performance metrics to manage projects
Element 8.3 Resolves conflict involving project team or stakeholders	
Performance Criteria	**Types of Evidence**
.1 Ensures that the team and stakeholders are fully aware of team rules	Documented team rules
.2 Recognizes conflict	Examples of conflict occurring within the project Team survey results
.3 Resolves conflicts	Examples of conflict resolution techniques used Feedback from team and stakeholders on satisfactory resolution of conflict

Table 3-3. Personal Competence—Managing (*concluded*)

9.0 Unit of Competence: Cognitive Ability	
Applies an appropriate depth of perception, discernment and judgment to effectively direct a project in a changing and evolving environment.	

Element 9.1 Takes a holistic view of project	
Performance Criteria	**Types of Evidence**
.1 Understands project stakeholders needs, interests, and influence for project success	Stakeholder analysis Communication plan aligned with stakeholders' needs Stakeholders' needs and objectives documented in project charter and project plan
.2 Understands how project actions impact other areas of the project, other projects, and organizational environment	Related external events included in project schedule Necessary documentation of project impact on organizational environment, if appropriate
.3 Understands both the formal and informal structure of organizations	Documented feedback from stakeholders on use of formal and informal organizational knowledge
.4 Understands organizational politics	Documented feedback from stakeholders on ability to operate within organizational politics
.5 Uses emotional intelligence to understand and explain others' past actions and current attitudes, and anticipate future behavior	Documented feedback on capturing verbal and non-verbal cues of the team Documented feedback from the team that the behaviors displayed are appropriate Documented feedback that different persuasion and motivation techniques were applied appropriate to each individual

Element 9.2 Effectively resolves issues and solves problems	
Performance Criteria	**Types of Evidence**
.1 Simplifies complexities for a complete and accurate analysis	Visual representations of project issues and interdependencies (lists, diagrams, relationship maps etc.) Analysis documents indicating use of techniques to break apart complex problems to find solutions
.2 Applies complex concepts or tools when needed	Issues log that provides methods proposed for analysis of complex issues Documented root-cause analysis, portfolio analysis, expert judgment etc. Documented analysis supporting issues resolution
.3 Applies lessons learned to resolve current project issues	Documentation of application of lessons learned to current project issues
.4 Aggregates multiple related issues to understand the complete picture	Summary reports or project scorecards outlining the relationships and linkages between project issues.
.5 Observes discrepancies, trends, and interrelationships in project data	Requests for information validation or confirmation Documented trend analysis

Table 3-4. Personal Competence—Cognitive Ability (*continued*)

Element 9.3 Uses appropriate project management tools and techniques	
Performance Criteria	**Types of Evidence**
.1 Understands PM tools and techniques	List of available tools and/or techniques
.2 Selects appropriate tools and/or techniques	List of selected tools and/or techniques Documented selection process and results
.3 Applies selected tools and/or techniques to project management	Outcomes achieved through use of tools and/or techniques
Element 9.4 Seeks opportunities to improve project outcome	
Performance Criteria	**Types of Evidence**
.1 Provides a framework to address opportunities and concerns	Lists of issues and associated opportunities or concerns distributed to all team members along with a clearly communicated process for updating the list Maintains issues log current and communicates changes/additions in it to all the stakeholders Meeting notes where issues were addressed documenting approaches and solutions identified Comparison between actions proposed and results obtained
.2 Looks for opportunities to improve project value or execution	Risk register showing opportunities Notes from brainstorming sessions, meetings, etc. where new opportunities were identified Documented suggestions in projects, or actions taken in a project related to the results obtained
.3 Seizes relevant opportunities as they emerge	Meeting notes where opportunities were analyzed Entries in change control process Examples of opportunities related to the moment they are presented during the evolution of the project
.4 Consolidates opportunities and passes them to the organization	Emails, meeting notes and other communication artifacts regarding project opportunities Documented proposals to clients or internal stakeholders indicating added value for pursuing identified opportunities Number of opportunities identified and pursued

Table 3-4. Personal Competence—Cognitive Ability *(concluded)*

10.0 Unit of Competence: Effectiveness	
Produces desired results by using appropriate resources, tools and techniques in all project management activities.	

Element 10.1 Resolves project problems	
Performance Criteria	**Types of Evidence**
.1 Employs appropriate problem solving techniques	Documented needs analysis (e.g., design inputs list) Documented feedback from stakeholders of problem solving techniques Documented use of proper knowledge management tools Issue log with resolution documentation
.2 Validates that proposed solutions resolve the problem and are within the project boundaries	Documented use of proper knowledge management tools Issue log with resolution documentation Documented feedback from stakeholder the problems were solved
.3 Chooses solutions that maximize project benefit and minimize negative impacts	Documented feedback from stakeholder stating the problems were resolved Documented impact of solution on project Documented external and/or environmental impact of solution

Element 10.2 Maintains project stakeholder involvement, motivation and support	
Performance Criteria	**Types of Evidence**
.1 Uses stakeholder communication to maintain stakeholder motivation	Communication plan Updates to stakeholder analysis Documented feedback from stakeholders stating that they felt motivated
.2 Constantly seeks opportunities to communicate project status and directions to meet the needs and expectations of stakeholders	Examples where the individual took an opportunity to communicate status Documented feedback from stakeholders on how their needs were met
.3 Includes experts in meetings and discussions to influence and obtain stakeholder support	Examples of how consensus and support were achieved on different issues Minutes from meetings where subject matter experts were invited for consultations with stakeholders
.4 Uses objectivity for consensus building	Documented use of best practices for making team decisions Examples of influencing biased team members toward objective position

Table 3-5. Personal Competence—Effectiveness *(continued)*

Element 10.3 Changes at the required pace to meet project needs	
Performance Criteria	**Types of Evidence**
.1 Adapts to changes in the project environment to minimize adverse project impacts	Documented feedback from stakeholders stating that the individual displayed a "can-do" attitude despite changes Documented risk mitigation activities
.2 Demonstrates flexibility towards changes that benefit the project	Risk registry updates identifying new opportunities Documented opportunities analysis Change requests
.3 Takes positive actions to capitalize on opportunities or to resolve present problems	Documented feedback from stakeholders that the project manager demonstrated an action-oriented and proactive approach Examples where the project manager resolved outstanding problems Project library with relevant documentation of technologies, techniques, or methods used during the project execution
.4 Enables a change-friendly environment by fostering continuous learning	Documented training recommendations for team members Project schedule includes time for team members to study new solutions, situations, or technologies Project library with relevant documentation of new technologies, techniques, or methods used during the project execution
.5 Acts as a change agent	Documented feedback from stakeholders regarding changes initiated or facilitated by project manager Documented feedback from stakeholders stating that the project manager demonstrated positive self-esteem and self-confidence

Element 10.4 Uses assertiveness when necessary	
Performance Criteria	**Types of Evidence**
.1 Takes initiative when required, assuming calculated risks to expedite project delivery	Feedback from stakeholders the PM took initiative when required Issue log with documented resolutions Issues escalation reports showing timely decision path
.2 Prevents inconclusive discussion, makes a decision, and takes appropriate action	Feedback from team on actions taken Examples where the PM declined a proposal without causing an argument and maintained cooperation Examples where the PM resolved a crisis by assessing the situation and offering decisive action
.3 Shows persistence and consistency in actions	Documented feedback from stakeholders stating that the PM showed persistence and consistency Meeting minutes, action item notes, or status reports showing decisions made Examples of maintaining motivation when faced with challenges
.4 Makes timely decisions based on facts while managing ambiguity	Decision memoranda or decision analysis documents demonstrating factual analysis of issues and prompt decision-making Issue log showing time from recording to resolution Issues escalation reports showing timely decision path

Table 3-5. Personal Competence—Effectiveness *(concluded)*

11.0 Unit of Competence: Professionalism	
Conforms to an ethical behavior governed by responsibility, respect, fairness, and honesty in the practice of project management.	

Element 11.1 Demonstrates commitment to the project	
Performance Criteria	**Types of Evidence**
.1 Understands and actively supports the project's and organization's mission and goals	Documented alignment of project goals and objective with organization's missions and strategy Examples where support was given when project goals differ from personal preferences Examples of defined project activities that support organizational goals
.2 Cooperates with all stakeholders to achieve project objectives	Examples of specific cooperative efforts to achieve project objectives Examples where team-building techniques were used to foster cooperation
.3 Makes sacrifices where necessary to move project forward	Examples of prior options taken for effective project execution while giving personal benefits a lower priority Examples where the PM demonstrated positive attitude while dealing with project challenges

Element 11.2 Operates with integrity	
Performance Criteria	**Types of Evidence**
.1 Adheres to all legal requirements	Feedback from stakeholders all legal requirements were met Documented log of legal requirements applied to the project with written stakeholder approval
.2 Works within a recognized set of ethical standards	Documented feedback from stakeholders stating that PM modeled ethical standards were used Documented feedback from stakeholders indicating the PM neither offered or accepted inappropriate payments or other items from any stakeholders
.3 Seeks to avoid and discloses any possible conflict of interests to all stakeholders	Example of truthful reporting of potential conflict of interests Organizational Conflict of Interest (OCI) statement and OCI plan
.4 Maintains and respects confidentiality of sensitive information	Documented feedback from stakeholders the individual maintains confidentiality Examples of project documentation that include the confidentiality or security level classification notice
.5 Respects the intellectual property of others	Documented agreements for reuse of protected intellectual property Documented searches for potentially applicable patents, trademarks, or copyrights Examples of copyright notice with source indication whenever protected intellectual property was used

Table 3-6. Personal Competence—Professionalism *(continued)*

Element 11.3 Handles personal and team adversity in a suitable manner	
Performance Criteria	**Types of Evidence**
.1 Maintains self-control in all situations and responds calmly	Examples where the PM felt strong emotions (such as anger or extreme frustration) but controlled them
	Uses stress-management techniques to control response, prevent burnout, and deal with ongoing stress
	Documented feedback from stakeholders indicating that the individual displayed self control
.2 Admits shortcomings and explicitly accepts responsibility for failures	Documented feedback from stakeholders where the individual actively listened to constructive feedback and acted on it
	Examples where the individual accepted responsibility for failure
.3 Learns from mistakes to improve future performance	Documented lessons learned
	Documented feedback from stakeholders stating that the individual learned from mistakes
	Examples where the individual analyzed his or her own performance to understand causes of mistakes and failures
Element 11.4 Manages a diverse workforce	
Performance Criteria	**Types of Evidence**
.1 Develops elements of trust and respect within the project environment	Documented feedback from team that the PM displayed an awareness of, respect for, and willingness to accommodate cultural differences
	Examples where the team celebrated achievements
.2 Ensures team's adherence to cultural issues, legal requirements, and ethical values	Document describing ethical standards and stakeholders' value systems
	Examples of consistently good moral judgment and behavior
	Documented analysis of applicable legislation, standards, and local customs relevant to the project
.3 Respects personal, ethnic, and cultural differences	Documented feedback from the team the PM respected personal, ethnic and cultural differences
	Examples where the PM valued the contribution of each team member
.4 Creates an environment of confidence and respect for individual differences	Documented feedback from team showing that they had confidence that the PM respected individual differences
	Examples where the PM created the conditions that motivated and enabled others to contribute their best

Table 3-6. Personal Competence—Professionalism *(continued)*

Element 11.5 Resolves individual and organizational issues with objectivity	
Performance Criteria	**Types of Evidence**
.1 Respects the organizational framework for running projects	Documented feedback from stakeholders that the individual respected privileges set forth for project managers in the organization
	Documented feedback from stakeholders that the project manager follows rules of collaboration and reporting within programs or portfolios of projects
.2 Balances individual interest with organizational interest	Documented feedback from stakeholders that the individual saw clear distinctions between individual and organizational interests
	Documented feedback from stakeholders that the individual adhered to PMI's professional code of conduct
.3 Assigns team members in an unbiased way to appropriate tasks	Skills assessment documentation indicating each team member's strength and weaknesses
	Responsibility Assignment Matrix (RAM) aligned with team member's skills assessment
	Examples of personnel assignment that allows them to grow by doing more than status quo

Table 3-6. Personal Competence—Professionalism *(concluded)*

Chapter 4

Developing Competence as a Project Manager

The purpose of this chapter is to show how the Performance and Personal Competencies defined in Chapters 2 and 3 can be used to facilitate the development of project management competence. The process recommended is for the continuous development of project management competence, as shown in Figure 4-1.

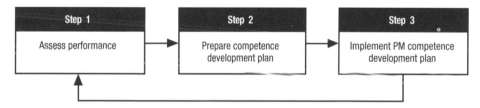

Figure 4-1. Competence Development Process

This process is intended to be used by project managers and organizations to assess project management performance with the aim of continuous skill improvement. The process is not intended to be a one-time assessment to identify or certify competent project managers but is intended to be used in an ongoing basis. The competence development process may be performed periodically to assess and improve project management competence. It is unlikely that a project manager would be reviewed against all the *PMCD Framework* performance criteria in one assessment as the competence development process is intended to be performed on an ongoing basis.

For Step 1 of the competence development process, the competence of the project manager is assessed using the *PMCD Framework* as the baseline competencies. The *PMCD Framework* is designed to apply generically to most project managers, regardless of the project's nature, type, size, or complexity. The purpose of Step 1 is to identify a project manager's areas of strength and to determine where further competence development is needed.

Strengths are identified and noted where performance is seen to meet or exceed the *PMCD Framework* performance criteria. Development needs, where performance results do not meet the *PMCD Framework* performance criteria, should also be recognized and noted. The results of the assessment can be recorded.

In Step 2, a competence development plan is prepared in light of the Step 1 assessment results. The plan prescribes activities to be undertaken by the project manager that are necessary to achieve the learning required.

In Step 3, the developmental activities planned in Step 2 are executed. These activities will need to take into account both the priorities and needs of the organization and of the project(s) underway. These development activities should be monitored and tracked against the competence development plan.

The entire process is then repeated as the overall competence of the project manager is further developed.

The competence development process allows development activities and the methods of assessment to be adapted to develop training or performance assessment requirements. The entry and exit points of this process will depend on the objectives of the project manager or organization the project manager is working for.

This chapter covers the following topics:

4.1 **Assessment Rigor**
4.2 **Step 1: Assess Performance**
4.3 **Step 2: Plan Competence Development**
4.4 **Step 3: Implement Project Manager Competence Development Plan**
4.5 **In Summary**

4.1 Assessment Rigor

The target audience for this process reflects a wide range of use, from individual self-assessment through organization-wide assessment, up to (but not including) certification-level assessment of *PMCD Framework*.

- Project managers
- Managers of project managers
- Members of a Project Management Office
- Managers responsible for establishing and developing project manager competence
- Educators teaching project management and other related subjects
- Trainers developing project management educational programs
- Consultants to the industry of project/program management
- Human resource managers
- Senior management

The *rigor* applied in the competence development process is *the level of thoroughness, intensity, breadth, and depth for the assessment* of the project manager's competence. The level of rigor followed in applying the competence development process may vary depending upon the audience and intended outcomes. The relative levels of rigor are explained in this chapter. An organization or project manager should use the concept of rigor relative to the importance of developing project management competence. If an organization requires a strong project management capability, it would use greater rigor in the competence development process to ensure a high caliber project management competence.

Rigor is important because if insufficient rigor is used for the intended application of the framework, the results are meaningless and time may be wasted. On the other hand, if more time and effort are used than called for, time is spent producing information that may never be used and the credibility of the process may be lost. Also, this may cause a bias against further assessment. For example, an assessor should not spend two days with a project manager assessing 200 performance criteria just to identify a two-day basic project management class to attend.

Low rigor competence assessment typically involves casual self-assessment or informal assessment against the competence criteria. Its primary use is in personal development planning and improvement. An appropriate subset of the *PMCD Framework* can also be useful for team assessment and risk avoidance as a part of project kick-off. The disadvantage of self-assessment is that individuals view their own skills inconsistently and their comparison to the baseline will vary. Some individuals know themselves very well; others do not. Some individuals hold themselves to a higher standard, resulting in a lower rating of competence. This can be compensated for by performing a self-assessment and having the assessment reviewed by a peer or manager.

An example of low rigor is when project managers may assess their competence as a personal exercise or prior to an assessment by a third party. The individuals may apply the process with less rigor and the collection of evidence may be done over an extended period. The individuals will compare their performance against the performance criteria specified in Chapters 2 and 3. This self-assessment may lead to a request for assistance to address a development need or an organizational assessment.

Medium rigor is less casual and adds an appropriate selection of the following elements to the assessment process:

- Review of the suggested types of evidence for each Performance and Personal Competence.
- 360° feedback, where feedback is provided from all around the subject.
- Interviewing the project manager and evaluating the evidence to gain an understanding of the effort and contribution.
- Specific recommendation of action items to work on.
- Reassessment after implementation of the development plan.

Medium rigor requires the person performing the assessment to have attained the necessary range of competencies to enable them to make an assessment of the performance. The assessor will require competence in the assessment process and an in-depth understanding of project management competence. In addition, medium rigor takes more time; as much as two to four times the amount of time as the low-rigor approach described above. Furthermore, the results are more repeatable and useful.

A *high-rigor* approach to assessment should be documented so that it will be repeatable and consistent when conducting other assessments and adds the following, where appropriate:

- Assessment by qualified, independent assessors, to allow better observation of the Personal Competencies of the person being assessed. This also allows specific recommendations of the action items to be documented.
- Preparation and assessor review of project documentation, where the person being assessed describes how he or she demonstrated each of the performance criteria in a recent project.
- Workshops or simulations may be used to distinguish between ability to convince and ability to perform.
- Careful recordkeeping of each assessment judgment and reconciliation of assessor differences in independent scoring. This is essential for legal reasons, as well as for assessor evaluation.

High rigor increases the assessment effort and the consistency of the results.

4.2 Step 1—Assess Performance

In this step, the performance of a project manager can be assessed using various methods described below in subsections based on the level of rigor. The project manager will gather evidence to be used in the assessment against the *PMCD Framework* performance criteria. The organization may also prescribe the qualitative, quantitative, and interpretive methods to be used and how evidence is collected and assessed.

To encourage the concept of continuous improvement of competency, the objective is for the evidence to demonstrate that the project manager meets or exceeds the baseline competence defined by the *PMCD Framework*. The acceptable level of output or performance will need to be defined against the evidence prior to the assessment. These assessment levels can be defined simply. Levels of performance could, for example, be expressed as:

- Below expectations or developing competence.
- Meets expectations or is competent.
- Exceeds expectations or highly competent.

Wherever there is a gap, it is necessary to describe the extent of the gap and to define the development required. If at any time during the assessment process there appears to be a gap in competence that is putting the project currently being managed at risk, the assessor may need to immediately initiate actions to address the gap.

The gaps can be viewed at dimension, unit, or element levels, or as detailed as the performance criteria level. Not all gaps have to be examined at the same level of detail. The gaps can be viewed holistically to give a multi-dimensional picture (as depicted in Figure 1-3), or gaps can be viewed individually to address specific development opportunities.

Upon completion of the assessment, a plan should be created to guide the individual and organization toward the agreed-upon goals and objectives. Organizations may want to strive to address the key areas that will provide them with maximum improvement benefits, rather than by attempting to focus on all of the possible issues at once.

When there are sufficient performance criteria gaps within an element or unit, the development activity may require a more comprehensive approach to address the gaps. The assessor needs to be aware that when using a holistic approach, strength in one area could obscure one or more gaps in other areas. Hence the need to recognize when to use a holistic versus detailed approach.

4.2.1 Assessment at an Organizational Level

If the assessment process is being applied across an entire organization, the method of evaluation may be quite formal with either medium or high rigor. The assessor may be the individual's manager, a senior peer, or an external assessor/consultant. In many organizations a third party is involved to provide a consistent approach across the organization and may be from a human resources or training division.

The remainder of this chapter will refer to an assessor. In the case of a self assessment, the assessor will be the project manager.

The assessor should meet with the project manager to discuss the assessment process and to perform the assessment. It is recommended that the project manager completes the competence assessment independently. This should be recognized as an important input to the meeting with the assessor.

Notes explaining the assessor's observations and the reasoning that led to their assessment findings will need to be recorded as input to the plan and for deploying appropriate development activities.

An organization may supplement the *PMCD Framework* with additional project manager competencies to meet local expectations of project professionals. There may be project type, industry or technology specific requirements of a project manager that an organization may choose to include. The organization may want to interpret the *PMCD Framework* to align with their own levels of seniority or positions.

4.2.2 Assessment Log

An assessment log can be used to record the assessment findings, indicating competence gaps at the performance criteria or element level. A sample assessment log is shown in Figure 4-2.

4.3 Step 2—Prepare Competence Development Plan

Once the assessment has been completed, a competence development plan should be created. It is important to use the information that has been gathered in Step 1 to address the development needs of the individual project manager and to build on the strengths.

The results of the assessment should be addressed in a timely manner as there may be items identified by the assessment that would warrant immediate corrective action. Furthermore, the plan should be prioritized to address areas that are most critical to the individual and organization. Once the areas have been prioritized, a realistic timeline for the plan needs to be established.

Element 1.1: Project defined by business and customer needs

Performance Criteria	Types of Evidence	Self Assessment	Reviewer Assessment
1.1.1 Demonstrates an understanding of the link between the project and the needs of the business	Clear, lucid description of the links between projects the individual has completed and the needs of the business	Meets Expectations	Meets Expectations
1.1.2 Establishes all key stakeholders business needs	Document describing business needs from a project the individual has successfully completed	Meets Expectations	Exceeds Expectations
1.1.3 Determines product/service characteristics using expert judgement as needed	Document defining customer requirements linked to a project plan the individual has used to deliver a successful project	Meets Expectations	Meets Expectations

Comment: This was performed well. The project manager not only initially established the needs and requirements but continued to reconfirm them throughout the project.

Element 1.2: Scope reflects business and customer needs and expectations

Performance Criteria	Types of Evidence	Self Assessment	Reviewer Assessment
1.2.1 Understands the scope of the project	A clear description of the scope	Meets Expectations	Meets Expectations
1.2.2 Frames high level project scope ensuring alignment with business and customer needs and expectations	Documented high leve scope, formal agreements with stakeholders	Meets Expectations	Meets Expectations

Comment: The scope was well documented. The organization has tools to assist the recording of scope and the project manager would benefit from learning how to use these tools.

Element 1.3: High level risks, assumptions and constraints are understood

Performance Criteria	Types of Evidence	Self Assessment	Reviewer Assessment
1.3.1 Establishes the high level assumptions and constraints for the project	Documented assumptions and constraints	Meets Expectations	Below Expectations
1.3.2 Identifies and understands the high level risks for the project		Meets Expectations	Exceeds Expectations
1.3.3 Quantifies the high level risks	List of quantified high level risks	Meets Expectations	Below Expectations

Comment: The standard tools were not used to gather and record risks. Some risks were identified but if the established risk identification process had been used a more comprehensive list of risk would have been identified.

Figure 4-2. Sample Assessment Log (continued)

Element 1.4: Key stakeholders identified and their needs are understood		Self Assessment	Reviewer Assessment
Performance Criteria	**Types of Evidence**		
1.4.1 Identifies all project stakeholders	Lists of key stakeholders	Meets Expectations	Meets Expectations
1.4.2 Conducts stakeholder analysis to identify key stakeholders and understand their agendas	A description of their needs/agendas	Meets Expectations	Exceeds Expectations
1.4.3 Identify high level communication requirements	Defined high level communication requirements	Meets Expectations	Meets Expectations
Comment: Performed satisfactorily.			

Element 1.5: Draft project charter available for review by key stakeholders		Self Assessment	Reviewer Assessment
Performance Criteria	**Types of Evidence**		
1.5.1 Develops a high level solution for the project	Documented high level solution	Meets Expectations	Meets Expectations
1.5.2 Establishes the key dates and deliverables to include in the project charter	Lists of dates and deliverables	Meets Expectations	Exceeds Expectations
1.5.3 Supports the preparation of the project charter	Draft charter for a project	Meets Expectations	Below Expectations
Comment: Although this was done, it could have been done better with the use of the standard project chart template and consulting other project managers who have done this before.			

Element 1.6: Project charter approved		Self Assessment	Reviewer Assessment
Performance Criteria	**Types of Evidence**		
1.6.1 Uses formal governance process to obtain sponsor approval and commitment	Approved project charter, with governance documentation for a project	Meets Expectations	Meets Expectations
1.6.2 Stores approved documents for future reference	Documents stored and accessible	Meets Expectations	Exceeds Expectations
Comment: Despite that it was a non-standard chart the project manager gained approval for the project chart.			

Figure 4-2. Sample Assessment Log (concluded)

By focusing on the high priority items, which are indicated as requiring additional development, a more effective plan can be implemented. Just as the work breakdown structure is an effective means of decomposing a large project into more manageable deliverables, the competence assessment helps to segregate the elements.

4.3.1 Ways of Addressing Development Needs

Addressing development needs can be done in a number of ways. This may depend on a number of aspects such as available resources, cost, and time. Selecting the best method will require some analysis. The following are learning environments that may be used to address development needs:

- **Mentoring**—A mentor can be assigned to a project manager as a "go to" person when the project manager needs assistance or would like to discuss project management issues. The mentor may or may not be the project manager's own line manager. The project manager can discuss issues or concerns with the mentor; seeking mentor advice on how to handle or address issues the project manager is experiencing. Mentoring works best where the project manager wants to address the development needs. Mentoring is usually driven by the project manager and is usually a long-term activity.
- **Coaching**—A competent coach can be appointed to work with the project manager to help him or her to learn from the coach's experience and to learn more about the project manager process, the organization in which he or she works, and its impact on it. Whereas training will bring learning from the experience of others, effective coaching will enhance the learning by the project manager's own experience.
- **Peer-to-Peer**—This usually happens when project managers have similar capabilities and can provide support to each other. This arrangement can create a particularly positive and supportive environment for two or more project managers. Occasionally, it may be necessary for a more experienced or senior project manager to also become involved to ensure alignment with best practice.
- **Role Playing**—Role playing can be appropriate when specific developments or behaviors need to be addressed. Participants use role playing to explore the human dynamics of project situations. The humor and drama from this activity enhances learning and the understanding of meaning.
- **On-the-Job Training**—A project manager can gain experience on 'live' projects to build confidence, gradually advancing the complexity and breadth of experience. This may mean assigning a project manager to a small or less complex project until he or she demonstrates comprehension of project management competence. This should not amount to allowing a project manager to fail, but should, nevertheless provide an opportunity for the project manager to learn. This arrangement should be structured and supportive.
- **Group Training**—This type of training can be deployed by an educational resource for a number of project managers who require the same development. For a consistent approach this is often used at entry-level training. More specific development needs would be addressed using a different method.
- **In-House Training**—An experienced project manager delivers this form of training within the organization. This is either a complete project management training course or specific training that has been identified as a deficiency within the organization.
- **CBT (Computer-Based Training)**—This is a form of training in which the training is programmed and presented using a computer system. This arrangement is suited to creating a learning experience for individual learners. Purchased training can be used at the project manager's pace and convenience (typically self-paced). Using a blended learning approach, CBT is deployed together with other learning experiences. CBT can also be used as convenient refresher material.
- **Individual Training**—This type of training can be used if there are one or more project managers who require training in a specific area and the resources are not readily available. There are a number of Registered Education Providers (REPs) available. A list of these resources and the particular topics that they cover is available on the Project Management Institute's website at www.pmi.org.

- **PMI®-Sponsored Programs**—PMI provides a wide range of training and educational programs. A list of these programs and the particular topics that they cover is available on PMI's website at www.pmi.org.
- **Public Education**—A number of post-secondary schools and colleges provide project management training. Certificate and degree courses (including post-graduate programs) in project management are also available.
- **Conferences**—A professional project manager will often discover great benefit from exposure to new and unfamiliar topics at conferences.

4.3.2 Competence Development Plan

In the development of a competency development plan, the assessor would be expected to work with the project manager to identify items such as: *PMCD Framework* reference, learning activity to address the identified gaps, target date to address the gap, and level to be achieved.

The competence development plan follows a performance assessment and lists the activities which are to be undertaken. In the example of a competence development plan (see Figure 4-3), each line represents a component of learning that indicates how the project manager will address the gap and which level the project manager is expected to achieve. When all items in the plan are combined, they represent the activities required to achieve an intended level of competence.

Line No.	Label (Known as)	PMCD Framework Reference	Learning Outcome (Behavior) Required	Learning Activity Type	Target Date	Mentor Name	Pre-Development	Level to be Achieved Post-Development
21	Action to influence	Personal 2.5.1	Continually reviewing where persuasion is likely to be needed and the method most likely to succeed	Mentoring/ coaching	December 2007	Arthur Wright	Below expectations June 16 2006	Exceeds expectations December 5 2007
22	Level of detail required to define the project scope	Performance 2.1.1	Develop the use of WBS to breakdown project scope	Training course on use of WBS	October 2006	n/a	Below expectations June 16 2006	Meets expectations October 2006

Figure 4-3. Example Section of a Competence Development Plan

The plan should include activities to address developmental areas and ways to leverage strengths, and should include actual activities, timing, costs and metrics. While ownership of the plan remains with the individual, most plans will have a sponsor within the organization. The sponsor may be the direct manager or a senior mentor. Proactively including the manager/sponsor/mentor in the monitoring of the plan provides an opportunity to ensure the career development is given their support.

4.4 Step 3—Implement Project Manager Competence Development Plan

Once the competence development plan is agreed upon between the project manager and the assessor, the plan can then be executed.

4.4.1 Completion of the Planned Activities

The project manager owns this plan and is accountable for delivering the outcomes. The project manager needs to execute this plan just as a project manager would execute a project plan.

While an organization may be involved in the development and support of a project manager's competence development plan, it remains the responsibility of the individual to ensure that the plan put in place is followed and the benefits are realized. The outcomes of the plan will allow the individual to improve their performance and reap the benefits in their career.

4.4.2 Monitor the Execution of the Plan

The monitoring of the plan should commence once there is an agreed framework for the plan. There may be cost associated with the execution of the plan and this needs to be approved and budgeted.

While the plan is being monitored it also needs to remain relevant. The situation surrounding the project manager may change; the current project may require a different type of support or may highlight a new strength. A particular activity may not be providing the necessary outcomes and may need to be realigned to better address a particular weakness.

The competence development plan should be monitored regularly with the sponsor. For each milestone in the plan, there must be measurable outcomes, which may include:

- Formal training
- Feedback from stakeholders
- Presentations to stakeholders
- Delivery of project outcomes
- Mentoring activities
- Networking professionally with peers

Collection of data against these outcomes will provide concrete evidence of progress. When an activity/outcome is complete, this needs to be reported against the plan and communicated to key stakeholders of the plan. The project manager should regularly conduct an informal review of the plan, at least once per month. Formal review of the plan should be performed on the completion of major milestones, phases, or projects and should be conducted with the manager/sponsor/mentor. Many organizations include this review as a major part of their performance management processes.

4.4.3 Support for the Plan

Successful completion of the competence development plan depends on the motivation of the project manager and the support given to the project manager. Within an organization this support comes from the immediate manager and senior peers. This support will need to be engaged and the relationship nurtured. Engagement requires an understanding of the plan, what it is, how it will be rolled out and what is needed to support the project manager. The role of the project manager is to introduce the plan to the people he or she expects support from, to explain the benefits expected, and to ensure that relevant stakeholders are kept up to date.

4.4.4 Evaluate the Execution of the Plan

Progress against the plan will be evaluated continually through the execution of the plan. When the planned actions have been completed, the project manager should be able to demonstrate that the identified development needs have been addressed. Now is the time for the individual to congratulate himself or herself and celebrate.

As with any plan that is executed, there also needs to be a formal review of the success of the plan to determine whether it really achieved the expected outcomes. Some of the questions that need to be asked include:

- Was the plan suitable?
- Did the plan deliver the outcomes needed?
- Was there sufficient support for the project manager and the plan?
- Were there activities that would have provided better outcomes?
- Can others now use the same plan?

4.5 In summary

The previous chapters of *PMCD Framework* defined the performance and personal competencies that, together with the Knowledge Competencies defined in the *PMBOK® Guide*—Third Edition, are considered required for a competent project manager. It was also indicated that each organization might customize the framework to its particularities, potentially using a subset of the competencies defined in this document and adding other competency dimensions important in their particular environment.

This chapter recommended an iterative process to develop competence as a project manager, where we assess the competence of project managers, plan competence development for the project managers, execute the competence development plan and then repeat the process.

Each iteration of the competence development plan should be treated as a project in itself. The project manager owns the plan and is accountable for delivering the outcomes. The project manager needs to execute the plan just as any other project plan would be executed. Successful completion of the competence development plan depends on the motivation of the project manager and the support given to the project manager by the senior project managers and peers.

The *PMCD Framework*—Second Edition has been developed to provide both individuals and organizations with guidance on how to assess, plan and manage the professional development of a project manager. Use of the framework will provide a structured approach to the continuing journey of competence development for individuals as well as organizations.

Appendix A

Second Edition Changes

The purpose of this appendix is to give a detailed explanation of the changes made to the *Project Manager Competency Development Framework* that was released in 2002 to create the *Project Manager Competency Development Framework*—Second Edition.

Structural Changes

The project team for the *PMCD Framework*—Second Edition was asked to update the document, taking into account the following:
- Research conducted by PMI through the Role Delineation Study culminating in the *PMP Examination Specification*
- Alignment with existing PMI Standards, in particular *A Guide to the Project Management Body of Knowledge (PMBOK® Guide)*—Third Edition
- Feedback from the marketplace on the 2002 document
- Possible submission to ANSI-for approval as Ameican National Standard

This resulted in the following structural changes (see Table A-1) and name changes (see Table A-2).:

Structural Changes: *PMCD Framework*—2002 Edition	Structural Changes: *PMCD Framework*—Second Edition
Nine Performance Competencc Units based on the Knowledge Areas from the *PMBOK® Guide*—2000 Edition	Five Personal Competence Units based on Performance Domains from the *PMP Examination Specification*
Performance Competence Elements of units based on *National Competency Standards for Project Management—Australian Institute of Project Management (AIPM)*	Performance Competence Elements of units based on *PMP Examination Specification* and expressed in outcomes
Six Personal Competence Units based on "Spencer Model"	Six Personal Competence Units further defined to include the *PMI Code of Ethics and Professional Conduct*
Section 4—Developing competence as a project manager was not seen as adding a great deal of value to the document	Chapter 4—Developing competence as a project manager includes a development framework and support to plan and develop ongoing project management competence improvement

Table A-1. Structural Changes

Name Changes: 2002 Edition	Name Changes: *PMCD Framework*—Second Edition
Section 2 **Performance Competencies** Project Integration Management Project Scope Management Project Time Management Project Cost Management Project Quality Management Project Human Resources Management Project Communications Management Project Risk Management Project Procurement Management	**Chapter 2** **Performance Competencies** Initiating a Project Planning a Project Executing a Project Initiating and Controlling a Project Closing a Project
Section 3 **Personal Competencies** Achievement and Action Helping and Human Service Impact and Influence Managerial Cognitive Personal Effectiveness	**Chapter 3** **Personal Competencies** Communicating Leading Managing Cognitive Ability Effectiveness Professionalism

Table A-2. Name Changes

Writing Styles

A style guide was used in order to guide the project team in using a standard, best practice approach. The style guide served as a detailed guideline for the team to use in the document development, review, and edit process and resulted in a consistent tone, structure, and vocabulary in the final document.

The team employed a five-step process in reviewing the document that included grammar and punctuation, content analysis, nomenclature, overall "look and feel" (including formatting and usability), and consistency of voice.

Chapter 1

Chapter 1 of the *PMCD Framework*—Second Edition provides an introduction to the concepts conveyed in the remaining chapters and has been modified to align with changes made to these chapters in the second edition.

In addition, a number of other changes were made to the chapter. The project team considered it important to clearly identify the target audience for the *PMCD Framework*—Second Edition within Chapter 1 and to provide an indication of who would be most likely to benefit from the standard.

A significant difference between the First and Second Editions of the *PMCD Framework* is the lack of detailed definition of knowledge competencies. This chapter provides an explanation for this deficit and a simpler view of the dimensions of competence.

The project team felt that the term "project success" has a number of connotations and that it is not necessarily always a product of project manager competence. It was therefore decided to remove the section on project success from Chapter 1.

The 2002 edition of the *PMCD Framework* references sources of information used for the edition. The second edition provides a more detailed overview of the alignment of the *PMCD Framework* with other PMI standards and publications.

The second edition simplifies and rationalizes the structure of the document. This is reflected in Chapter 1 with one figure being used to illustrate the structure of both chapters two and three. The numbering system used within these chapters is significantly simpler than the previous edition and does not, therefore, require detailed explanation.

PMCD Framework - 2002 Edition	PMCD Framework - Second Edition
Target audience not identified.	Identification of Target Audience.
Detailed definition of dimensions of competency including knowledge.	Simple representation of dimensions of competence.
Discussion on the relationship of Project Manager Competency and Project Success.	Section on Project Success removed.
Acknowledgement of sources used for the edition.	Alignment of PMCD Framework with PMI standards and publications.
Detailed explanation of structure and numbering system used within the document.	Simple representation of rationalized structure.

Table A-3. Chapter 1 Changes

Chapter 2

Chapter 2 has been completely restructured as a result of the role delineation study findings documented in the *PMP Examination Specification*. The results show the membership view of project management from a process group perspective and not from a knowledge area perspective. This information resulted in the reduction of Performance Competence Units descriptions to five. This also aligns with what is seen as good practice in defining competencies. The five Performance Competence Units are based on five of the six Performance Domains defined in the PMP Examination Specification. The sixth Performance Domain specified in the PMP Examination Specification—*Professional and Social Responsibility*—is not included as a performance competence but is included in Chapter 3 as a Personal Competence. The *PMP Examination Specification* was also used to define the elements of each unit. The wording however was changed so that each element was described as an outcome to be achieved rather than a process to follow. Each element is further broken down in performance criteria developed by the team using the *PMCD Framework*—2002 Edition, the *PMP Examination Specification* and existing PMI standards. The achievement of each of the performance criteria ensures that the outcome specified in the element will be delivered. In order to establish achievement of the performance criteria, the project team defined the types of evidence that could demonstrate achievement of each criteria. In Chapter 2, a "one for one" approach was taken between performance criteria and types of evidence but this should be seen as an example only, there may be other types of evidence that can demonstrate compliance.

PMCD Framework - 2002 Edition	PMCD Framework - Second Edition
Nine Performance Competencies from the PMBOK® Guide—2000 Edition	Five Performance Competencies from the PMP Exam Specification
Elements from AIPM PM Competencies	Elements from PMP Exam Specification
Performance Criteria from the PMBOK® Guide—2000 Edition	Performance criteria developed by project team from PMCD Framework—2002, the PMBOK® Guide—Third Edition and the PMP Exam Specification
Examples of assessment guidelines developed by project team	Types of evidence developed by project team, typically "one for one" with performance criteria

Table A-4. Chapter 2 Changes

Chapter 3

Chapter 3 also evolved from the previous edition, moving further from the initially used Competency Dictionary (known as the Spencer Model) developed by Lyle and Signe Spencer (1993). The new competency units are the result of a deeper understanding of the specific Personal Competencies required for project management. The most visible evolution in the definition of Personal Competencies for a project manager is the new Competence Unit titled Professionalism, supporting PMI's *Code of Ethics and Professional Conduct* as well as the Professional and Social Responsibility section from the *PMP Examination Specification.*

The Second Edition includes six Personal Competence Units, as did the 2002 Edition. The units' names have been shortened and their content area better separated, aligning with best practices in defining competency frameworks. However, due to the subjective nature of personal competencies, there might be elements that have characteristics of more than a single unit. In such cases, a judgment call was made regarding most appropriate placement of such element, acknowledging its other characteristics as well.

Most competency elements were preserved from the 2002 Edition (in some instances consolidated for clarity), some were added and a few were deleted. They were regrouped into the new Competency Units based on their usage and relationships specific to project management. Each element is further broken down in performance criteria representing behaviors showing the presence of the competence element. The achievement of each of the performance criteria is established through the existence of one or more of the types of evidence listed. The types of evidence are for exemplification only as each organization might use other similar documents or facts to demonstrate the accomplishment of a performance criterion.

PMCD Framework–2002 Edition	*PMCD Framework*–Second Edition
Six Personal Competence Units: • Achievement and action • Helping and human service • Impact and influence • Managerial • Cognitive • Personal effectiveness	Six Personal Competence Units: • Communicating • Leading • Managing • Cognitive ability • Effectiveness • Professionalism
Competence elements from Spencer Model	Competence elements derived from *PMCDF*–2002 Edition, the *PMBOK® Guide*–Third Edition, the *PMP Exam Specification*, and the PMI *Code of Ethics and Professional Conduct*
Performance criteria from Spencer Model and the *PMBOK® Guide*–2000 Edition	Performance criteria developed by project team from *PMCD Framework*–2002 Edition, the *PMBOK® Guide*–Third Edition, the *PMP Exam Specification* and the PMI *Code of Ethics and Professional Conduct*
No types of evidence	Sample types of evidence that could demonstrate, alone or in conjunction with other evidences, the presence of the desired behavior indicated by a performance criterion.

Table A-5. Chapter 3 Changes

Chapter 4

Chapter 4 has been completely rewritten coincident with the restructure of the rest of the document. The objective of this chapter, unlike the 2002 edition's focus on the attempt to achieve a certain level of competence, was to use the *PMCD Framework* to assess the level of competence demonstrated in the project managers' performance. The purpose of this is to promote continuous improvement rather than trying to reach some arbitrary level of competence.

PMCD Framework–2002 Edition	*PMCD Framework*–Second Edition
Five-stage approach: ● Stage 1: Determine applicable elements and performance criteria ● Stage 2: Determine desired levels of proficiency ● Stage 3: Assessment ● Stage 4: Addressing gaps in competency ● Stage 5: Progress toward competence	Three-step approach: ● Step 1: Assess performance ● Step 2: Prepare competence development plan ● Step 3: Implement PM competence development plan

Table A-6. Chapter 4 Changes

Appendix B

Evolution of the *PMCD Framework*

The PMI Standards Committee sponsored the Project Management Competency (PMC) project in 1998 to work on a competency framework for project managers. The purpose of the project was to develop a project manager competency development framework that described the competencies likely to lead to effective project manager performance across contexts. The competency framework was to be used for the *professional development* of project managers rather than in selection or performance evaluation.

The Standards Committee recognizes that professionalism in project management is greatly facilitated by a project management competency framework that:
* is generally accepted throughout the profession.
* provides guidance to both individuals and organizations regarding how to manage the professional growth of a project manager.
* addresses a full range of project types from small and simple to large and complex.

Consequently, in late 1998, the PMI Standards Committee asked for volunteers to develop a *standard* outlining a project manager competency development framework and sponsored the Project Manager Competency (PMC) project team. The *PMCD Framework* was to identify and define some of the key dimensions of effective performance, the competencies that likely impact performance, and the contingencies likely to influence the extent to which a particular competency had an impact on project manager performance. A volunteer team was assembled and, during the course of the next year, worked on refining the project's scope, reviewing the literature, and starting to develop the basic framework and definitions outlining project manager competency.

In the fall of 2000, PMI's certification department published the *Project Management Professional (PMP) Role Delineation Study* and the *Project Management Experience and Knowledge Self-Assessment Manual*. The PMC core team reviewed this work in comparison to the elements and criteria contained in the draft *PMCD Framework*. A decision was made to revise the elements of competence and performance criteria contained within the *PMCD Framework* to align with the works published by PMI certification. The PMC core team, with support from the PMI Project Management Standards Program, conducted an open working session at *PMI 2000*. Additional input was solicited from those attending the session regarding the completeness and usefulness of the draft *PMCD Framework*. Input indicated that the draft *PMCD Framework* would serve as a useful resource for those working to develop the competence of project managers within their organizations.

The draft of the *PMCD Framework* was submitted to the PMI Project Management Standards Program Team in March 2001 for consideration as an *Exposure Draft* to be circulated among PMI membership and other affected parties. Following approval by the Standards Program Team, the proposed exposure draft was submitted for formal review to six other knowledge experts. The *PMCD Framework* project team evaluated the comments from these six reviewers and the Standards Program Team. A final draft was submitted to the Standards Program Team and approved for this exposure draft.

The Exposure Draft was submitted for public review on 1 October 2001, with an exposure closure on 3 December 2001. During this period 154 comments were received. Each idea proposed during the review was evaluated and decisions made as to whether to incorporate the recommendation into this version of the *PMCD Framework*. All comments that the project team accepted for the current version have been incorporated.

B1. *PMCD Framework*—1ˢᵗ Edition Project Team

Core Team Members

Scott Gill, MBA, PMP—Project Manager
David Violette, MBA, PMP—Deputy Project Manager
William C. (Clifton) Baldwin, MS
Christopher Bredillet, DSc, MBA
Chris Cartwright, PMP
Paul Fiala, MS
Kenneth J. Stevenson, MS

Review Team Members

Sumner Alpert, MBA, PMP
Dennis Bolles, PMP
Craig Carvin, PMP
Gilbert Guay
Hans Jonasson, PMP
Jacob Stranger Kgamphe
Barbara Marino, MPM, PMP
Kevin Porter, PMP
Angela Sheets
Shoukat M. Sheikh, MBA, PMP
Alberto Villa, MBA, PMP
Thomas Williamson, PMP
Xiaolan Wang

Initial PMCD Framework Project Team

Janet Szumal, PhD—Project Manager
Nicola Barron
Christopher Bredillet, DSc, MBA
Chris Cartwright, PMP
John Chiorini, PhD, PMP
Rob Cooke, Ph.D.
Lynn Crawford
Russ Darnell, MS
David Denny, PMP
Karen DiPierro
Kathleen Donohue
Dick Drews, PMP
Ellen Edman

David Garbitt
Larry Goldsmith, PMP
William C. Grigg, PE, PMP
Brad King
Alan Kristynik, PMP
Rose Mary Lewis, PMP
Lawrence Mack, PE, PMP
Barbara Marino, MPM, PMP
Dave Maynard, MBA, PMP
Vrinda Menon, PMP
Richard Ray
Paul Rust, PMP
Philip Sharpe, PMP
Gregory Skulmoski
Cyndi Stackpole, PMP
Ken Stevenson, MS
Dick Waltz, PMP
Greg Willits, PMP
Peter Wynne
Frank Yanagimachi

Selected Reviewers of Pre-Exposure Draft

These volunteers provided specific evaluations and comments on the pre-exposure draft. The project team and the PMI Standards Program Team considered their input in the development of the Exposure Draft.

James P. Henderson, PhD
Normand Pettersen, PhD
Lynn Crawford
Tomas Linhard
T.I. Morris
Brian Hobbs

Reviewers of Exposure Draft

Kim Colenso, PMP
Judy VanMeter
Nigel Blampied
Brian Gaspar
Portia Saul, PMP
Crispin "Kik" Piney, Bsc, PMP
Brian Hobbs, PMP
Cyndi Stackpole, PMP
Jody A. McIlrath
Greg Skulmoski
George Sukumar, PE

B2. Evolution of the *PMCD Framework*—Second Edition

The *PMCD Framework*—Second Edition project started in mid-2004 under the project management of Chris Cartwright, one of the core team members of the first edition. The initial project team of approximately 80 began reviewing the first edition of the standard and the various PMI publications that were linked to project management competence. During the life of the project, the team grew to over 380 volunteers.

The standard was restructured along the lines of the *PMP Exam Specification*, based on project charter direction from PMI. The team also took the opportunity to expand the document to cover three levels of project managers. A first draft of the standard was created by late 2005. This consisted of a framework to assess and develop project coordinators, project managers, and senior project managers. While this expanded the scope of the charter, the team believed that the standard would have a greater value to the profession.

In early 2006, PMI directed the team to focus solely on the project manager, leaving the other levels of competency development to future projects. The charter for the *PMCD Framework* was strengthened and a new core team was developed with the addition of a deputy project manager to drive adherence to the charter. The core team consisted of:

- Lyn Windsor—Introduction and Chapter 1;
- George Jucan—Chapter 3, covering Personal Competencies
- Paul Osman—Chapter 4 on developing competence.

This left the project manager, Chris Cartwright, as the chapter lead for Chapter 2 on Performance Competence. The core team also included team members with responsibility for specific functions necessary to complete the second edition:

- Jen Skrabak took responsibility for the edit team;
- Mike Reid headed up the integration team;
- Neelesh Ajmani assumed the role of volunteer administration and general HR.

The team welcomed Mike Yinger to the role of deputy PM, who brought a great deal of experience and drive to the engine room of the project.

The team established regular teleconferences and set up groups of volunteers to support the work of developing the four chapters. Some of the chapter team members went far beyond what is normally expected of volunteers and they are recognized as significant contributors in Appendix C.

Over a number of months, the various teams developed their chapters using regular teleconferences. The decision was made to bring the core team together to review the chapters at a face-to-face meeting. The core team consisted of five members from North America and three members from Australia. The first face-to-face meeting was held in May 2006.

While the use of modern technology allows us to work in virtual teams, there is still no better way to develop teamwork than to meet in person and get to know the faces associated with the names. One lesson learned from the first face-to-face meeting was to have this type of meeting early in the project to build the team focus and bond the team. The results of the meeting were taken back to the chapter teams and each chapter was revised using input from the meeting. The integration and edit teams provided input as to style and coverage and this was also included in the chapter edits.

The draft was now ready for a complete team review. Each team member was asked if they wished to participate and a formal review team was established. In the formal PMI Standards Department process for this stage of the project, there can be up to four different types of reviews to manage the quality of the final document. There will be an internal review, there may be a subject matter expert (SME) review, there will be a Members Advisory Group (MAG) review, and finally there will be the exposure draft (ED) review, which is open to the world-at-large. When the revision was ready for the project team review, it was forwarded to PMI Standards for the internal edit, where the decision was made that the document was comparatively ready for Exposure Draft and, consequently, the decision was made by PMI Standards to administer three of the reviews in parallel. The core team agreed and ran the internal team review, the SME review and the MAG review at the same time.

The reviewers made a substantial contribution to the document, providing over 2700 suggestions for improvements to the document. As this stage of the process was the first opportunity many of the review team had to see the complete document; the internal project team review was especially helpful. The chapter teams then incorporated the suggestions where necessary and the core team had a second face-to-face meeting to review the complete document. This was a particularly arduous and intensive meeting, with much discussion and debate. The revised draft of the standard was then forwarded to PMI Standards Department for the Exposure Draft (public) review. The normal ED process was followed and this provided approximately 285 comments from the membership. While this number is low compared to other standards, the team believes it reflects the quality of the work done by all previous reviewers. More than 80% of the ED comments were included in the final draft of the document.

While the final draft of the *PMCD Framework*—Second Edition meets its charter's stated goal (to provide necessary information to the project manager who is at the PMP® level, the team believes there is a need to expand the framework in future editions to include those levels which are outside of the PMP® level, both above and below. This and future frameworks may be used by organizations as a development path for project staff.

Several steps were taken in the HR processes of the team to coordinate the large number of volunteers. The core team put in place a process for induction and polled each new arrival for their interests in allocating them to a suitable task. A regular newsletter was also implemented to communicate to all team members regarding progress and achievements. It is gratifying to this project team that its efforts to maintain the energy and enthusiasm of so many volunteers have been recognized by the PMI Standards Department as an appropriate template for changes to the overall Standards project team creation and maintenance process.

The core team of the *PMCD Framework* project would like to acknowledge the support provided by the team at PMI Standards, from the Standards Manager and from a number of Standard Project Specialists. This support was greatly appreciated and helped us all deliver the best standard that we could.

Appendix C

Contributors and Reviewers of the *Project Manager Competency Development Framework—* Second Edition

This appendix lists, alphabetically within groupings, those individuals who have contributed to the development and production of the *Project Manager Competency Development Framework—Second Edition.* No simple list or even multiple lists can adequately portray all the contributions of those who have volunteered to develop the *Project Manager Competency Development Framework—Second Edition.* Appendix B describes specific contributions of many of the individuals listed below and should be consulted for further information about individual contributions to the project.

The Project Management Institute is grateful to all of these individuals for their support and acknowledges their contributions to the project management profession.

C1. Project Manager Competency Development Framework—Second Edition Project Core Team

The following individuals served as members, were contributors of text or concepts, and served as leaders within the Project Core Team (PCT):

Chris Cartwright, PMP, *Project Manager*
Michael A. Yinger, MBA, PMP, *Deputy Project Manager*
Neelesh Ajmani, MBA, PMP
George Jucan, MSc, PMP
Paul Osman, PMP
Michael R. Reed, PMP
Jen L. Skrabak, PMP, MBA
J. Lyn Windsor, PMP

C2. Significant Contributors

Significant contributors supported key activities for the update to the *Project Manager Competency Development Framework*—Second Edition including editing and sub-team participation in project efforts such as Content, Authoring, Quality, Communications and Research subteams. The update project's significant contributors offered depth of knowledge and insight as Subject Matter Experts (SME) in their fields of practice. In addition to the members of the Project Core Team, the following individuals provided significant support, input or concepts:

Jaideep Agrawal, MBA, PMP
Gerard Aroquianadane, MBA, PMP
David Baker, MPA, PMP
Robert S. Banks, PMP
Nishu Bansal
Nathaniel Barksdale, Jr. PhD, PMP
Marcos Diclei Barros, PMP
Cindy Beck
Damien Bolton, PMP
Kevin Bourke, PMP
Terry Boyd, PhD, PMP
Melissa Fawn Bull
Raul Calimlim, MSSE, PMP
Anthony R. Corridore, PMP
Paramita Debbarman, PMP
Tracy Dixon, PMP, MBA
Mark Lester Dy, PMP
Stacy A. Goff, PMP
Pamela Brettmann-White, MBA, PMP
Priyesh Gopalakrishnan, PMP
Shyam Kumar G, PMP
Morgan E. Henrie, PhD, PMP
Bernard A. Holmes, CGFM, PMP
Kevin J. Hunziker, PMP
Rashed Iqbal, PhD, PMP
Puja Kasariya, PMP
Rod Koelker, MSc, PMP
Richard P. Krulis, PMP
Robin E. Kuczera
Anil Kumar, PMP
Dennis Lakier, PEng, PMP
Xiaosong Liu, PMP
Juan J. Monroy Lopez
Ganesh Malgikar, PMP
Lynn Qin Mu, B.Comm, PMP
Raja Sekhar Nerella, BE, PMP
Dumitru I. Oprea, PhD, DrHC
Beth Ouellette, MBA, PMP
Crispin "Kik" Piney, PMP
Martin Price, BSc, APMP
Prabhushankar Rajamani
Priscilla Rhaich'al, Honours BA
Lisa Rockwood
Rosalyn C. Samonte, PMP, CBCP

Martyn Scott, MA, PMP
Prakash Sharma, MBA, MBB
Rachna Sharma, PMP
Rachna Sharma, PMP
Gary J. Sikma, PMP, MBA
Anca E Slusanschi, MSc, PMP
Paul Steinfort, PMP, FIEAust
Susan J. Strople, PMP
Rocco Tellier, PMP
Prem Kiran Udayavarma, PMP
Derek H.T. Walker, PhD, MSc
Kyle S. Wills, PMP
Lucia Wong, MBA, PMP
Al Zeitoun, PhD, PMP

C3. *Project Manager Competency Development Framework*—Second Edition Project Team Members

In addition to those listed above, the following team members provided input to and recommendations on drafts of the *Project Manager Competency Development Framework—Second Edition*:

Aref Abouzahr, MBA, Eng
Abha Abraham
Tarek Abuelnaga, MBA, PMP
Anurag Agrawal, MTech, PMP
Imran Ahmed, PMP
Bob Aiken, PMP
Rajdeep Ajmani
Jessica Alcantara, PMP
Gustavo Adolfo Ortega Alvarado, Eng, PMP
Ahmed Samy Amer, PMP
Mauricio Arantes de Andrade
Lionel Andrew, MBA, ISP
Louisa Amalia Andrianopoulos, MSc
Guna Appalaraju
Cindy K. Archer-Burton, JD, PMP
Gabriel Arise, MBA, PMP
Kannan Arunachalam, BE (Hons), PMP
Anubhav Asthana
Scott T. Bable, PMP
Louis Bahrmasel
Joan Barnes-Weatherton
Richard Bates, PMP
Alan Bezuidenhout
Sanjay Bhaskaran, PMP
Rajat Bhatnagar, MS, PMP
Kaushik Bhowal MS, PMP
John A Blakely, MS, PMP
Gayle Armstrong Blizzard
Wallace "Bo" Bohanan MBA, PMP
Rakesh Boonlia, MBA
Roberta C. Bonsall, PMP

Diego Ramalho Bortolucci
Ann Abigail Bosacker, PMP
Connie Bouhaik, PMP
Adrienne L. Bransky, PMP
Rufus Earl Branson
Liz Brown, PMP
Mark Brenon
Terrance P. Bullock, PMP
James Burkholder, ASQ-CSSBB, PMP
Dawn Cain
Darlene F. Calvert, PMP
Marcia Carrere, PMP
Roberto C. Cavalcante, PMP
Daniel Thomas Cedar
Herman Chan, PMP
Subramanian Chandramouli
Chih-Wu Chang, MS, PMP
Rachel Chang, MA, PMP
Sourabh Chatterjee, CSQA, PMP
Rakesh N. Chauhan, MSc, PMP
Vijay Kumar Chemuturi, PMP
Amitabh Choudhary, PMP
Bhaskar Chowdhury, PMP
Victor Chu, PMP
Catherine S. Cockrell
Johanne H. Comeau, MGP, PMP
Miguel A. Conway, CISA, PMP
Ronald C. Cook, PMP
Thomas J. Cornish, PMP
Mario Damiani, PMP
Debabrata Das, PMP
Saji V. Dasan, SSBB, PMP
Hemang S. Dave
Beverly E. Davis
Stephanie E. Dawson, PMP
Vipul Dekhtawala, PMP
Andrea Delle Piane, PMP
Marcel A. Derosier
Rosaria DeNova, PMP
Anand Devulapalli
Sham Dhage
Pankaj Dhasmana
Rajesh Dhuddu, PMP, MFM
Mihai Diaconescu, PMP
Liam P. Dillon
Jorge Dominguez, PMP
Anagha Donde, PMP
Hemanta K. Doloi, PhD
Lloyd Russell Duke, Jr.
Thomas R. (Randy) Dunson, MBA, PMP
Richard Egelstaff, MBA (Adv), PMP
Kenith W. Ehalt

Srimal S. Ekkadu, PMP
Gregory Ellett
Michael E. Engel
Ruben D. Espinoza
Linda R. Finley, VP, CIO
Daniela Medeiros Firmono
Klaus Fremmelev, PMP
Arun Gajapathy, PMP
Mary M. Ganous
Cindy J. Genyk, MSCIT, PMP
Robert M Gerbrandt, CD, PMP
Edgar Gerke, PMP
Farrukh Ghaffar, PMP
Eyad Awni Ghosheh
Silvio H. Giraldo Gomez, CBCP, PMP
Robert Goodhand, PMP
Lata Gopinath, MS, PMP
Clifford G. Graham
Jeff Greenstreet, PMP
Keith Grindstaff, PMP
Daniel (Dana) Grove
Sirisha Gullapalli
Joanne Gumaer, PMP
Pooja Gupta
Ravi S Gupta, PMP
Brooke Hairston, MBA, PMP
Carl G Halford, MAPM, PCIRM
Cheryl L. Harris-Barney, MPM
Michael P. Hatheway, PMP
Graham S. Heap
Megan Heath
Hoon Hoon Heng, PMP
Sebuliba Herman
Celestine Hicks, PMP
Alan Chi Keung Ho
Eberhard Hoffmann, PMP
Roderick Holland, MBA, PMP
Stephen Martin Holland
Ahmed Hussein Aly, MBA, PMP
Michael Idoko, PMP
Anshoom Jain, MBA, PMP
Pawan Jalan, CPA, PMP
Chandrasekaran Jayaraman, PMP
Michelle Jehsus, PMP
M. Aamir Jelani
Raj Kumar Jhajharia, PMP
Lori Johnson, PMP
Gerard Joseph, MBA, PMP
Aadham Junaidallah, PMP, CISA
Alex Kangoun
Faisal Karim, PMP
Muruganand Karthikeyan, PMP

Kesava Reddy Kasireddy
Ramakrishna Kavirayani, PMP
Sahin Kaya, PMP
Gaurish Kerkar, PGDIM, PMP
Dilip Khadilkar, PMP
Moiz A. Khan, CISSP
Muhamman Kamran Khan
Manoj Khanna
Daniel Kim
Christopher C. King, PMP
Alan Ko, MBA, PMP
Takanoubu Kohinata
Sitarama Kota, M.Tech, PMP
Mahesh Krishnamoorthy, MBA, PMP
Raghuraman Krishnamurth
Ramesh Kulandaivel, MBA, PMP
Saravana Bhavan Kulandaivel
S. Adarsh Kumar, PMP
Mohan Kumar, MS, PMP
Prashant Kumar, PMP
Polisetty V.S. Kumar, CISSP, PMP
S. Suresh Kumar
Karthikeyan Kumaraguru, MS, PMP
Daniel G. Kushnir, MSc, PMP
Carla Lee, PMP
Craig Letavec, MSPM, PMP
Carol Ann Levis, PMP
Su-Che (David) Liao
Harshavardhan Limaye, CPIM, PMP
Sajith Madapatu, CSSMBB, PMP
Krishna Malladi, CSQE, PMP
Suresh S. Malladi, PMP
Manz Joachim, PhD, PMP
M. L. Marchwinski, MBA
Pietro Marini, PMP
Photoula Markou-Voskou, PMP
Lou Marks, PMP
Sucharitha R. Maroju, M.Tech, PMP
Andrew L. Marshall
Nancy J. Mather, PMP
Andrew McKnight, PMP
Jorge L. Mejia
Joanne Miles
Kimberlee Miller, MBA, PMP
Muhammad Aslam Mirza, MBA, PMP
Gaurav Mittal, BTech, PMP
Marcos Alberto Mochinski, PMP
Lori Monkaba
Alan F. Moore, MBA, PMP
Rajesh More
Chiara Moroni, PMP
Aaron Morrison

Chenoa Moss, MS ISE, PMP
Brenda M. Moten, MAOM, PMP
Anil Mudigal, PMP
Mustafa A. Mukhtar, CCE
Suman Munshi, PGDCA, MBA IT
Anand Murali
Subramanian N, PMP
Sainath Nagarajan, MISM, PMP
Jagadish Nagendra, PMP
Biju Nair, PMP
Hari Krishna Nallure, MBA
Alexandre B. Nascimento, MBA, PMP
Abanis Nayak
Beth Negash, MPM, PMP
Paul Nordick, MBA, PMP
Michael O'Connor, MS, PMP
Gethsemani Palacios, PMP
Marisa F. Paladino
Timothy J. Papich MS, PMP
Bobby K. Paramasivam, BSMechEng, PMP
Vikram Paramasivan MBA, PMP
Kandarp Patel
Mridul Paul, MS, PMP
Randy L. Peeler, PMP
Ken Perry, MBA, PMP
Sitarama Chakravarthy Peruvel, MS, PMP
See Hua Phang
Paul M. Pond, MBA, PMP
Indira Prasad
Thomas J. Price, PE, PMP
Diana Prkacin
Claude Prudente, PMP
Rajwardhan Purohit, PMP, ITIL
Alison Rabelo, PMP
Angela Ragin
Angela Rahman, MS, PMP
Pathma Raj, MBA, PMP
Noshaba Raja
Aditya Rajguru, PMP
Krishna Ramaiah, PMP
Sameer Ramchandani, PMP
Houri Ramo, MS
Richard G. Ranney, MBA, PMP
Amburkar Ellappa Rao, MTech, PMP
Mahendra Singh Rathore, CISA, PMP
James P. Reid, MSc, MBA
Igor Reznik
Robert Rider, PMP
Rick Ringold, MBA, PMP
Pradyot Sahu
Anne Marie M. Saint Felix, PMP
Muhammad Salman Abid

Stanley Samuel, MBA, PMP
Sathyam Sankaran, PMP
Uthaya Prakash Santhanam
Udayan Sathe, MBA. PMP
Mamta Saxena, MBA, PMP
Terry A. Schmidt, PE, PMP
Ronald G. Schroll, MEd, PMP
John Schmitt, CSSMBB, PMP
Tufan Sevim
N. K. Senthilkumar, PMP
Viresh Shah
Sanina Shen, CISSP, PMP
Syed A. Sherazi (Hassan)
Ganesh Vinayak Shevade
Danny Shields, MS
Nancy (Nikki) A. Shields
Subrina Mei-Jing Shih, CPIM, PMP
Jayant Sinha, MBA, PMP
Rachanee Singprasong, MComm, PMP
Amandeep Singh, MCA, PMP
Subbakaran Singh, MBA, PMP
Atul Sinha, PMP
Som N. Sinha, MBA,PMP
Bhuvaneswari Sivasubramanian
Zdzisław S. Sławacki, MBA, PMP
Penny Smith, PMP
Michael J. Smith, PMP
Stephanie Snyder, PMP
Jason Lee Sneed
Sadanand Sonar, PMP
Lakshminarasimhan Srinivasan, MBA(Fin), PMP
Das Subhra
S. S.Venkata Subramanian, CISI, PMP
Gavin T. Sudhakar, CSSBB, PMP
Stuart Summerville
George Sunil
Lata Suresh
Biju G. Syamata
Mahta Taghizadeh, MSc
Kiran K Talasila, MBA, PMP
Terry Tanner, MScPM, PMP
Muhammad Tariq, SE, MBA
Sandhya Tayal, PMP
Mei-Hui, Teng, MSc, PMP
Lee Tian
Lee Towe, MBA, PMP
Melissa Ann Townshend, PMP
Savyasachi Tumkur, PMP
Anupam Upadhyay
Reddy Urimindi, PhD, PMP
Marianne Utendorf
Rajesh Vaidyanathan, PMP

Narayanan Veeriah, CFA, PMP
Swapna Veldanda
Sreedhar Vellamena, PMP
Sriram Venugopal, PMP
Michael Villani
Ramesh Vinakota
Vipin K. Viswan
Jyoti Wadhwa, MS
Andrew D. Warrender, MAPM, PMP
Kevin R. Wegryn, CPM, PMP
Greg Wilde, MS, PMP
Richard Earl Williams
Nancy L. Wirtz
Albert Mun On Wong
Lai Chi Wong, PMP
Tonya Woods, PMP
Michael A. Wright, Sr., CBA, PMP
Zhen Ning Wu, PMP
Kyle Xie, MSc, PMP
Rambabu (Bobby) Yarlagadda, MBA, PMP
Lijun Yi, MBA, PMP
Zoubair Zachri
Shakir Zuberi, MBA, PMP

C4. Final Exposure Draft Reviewers and Contributors

In addition to team members, the following individuals provided recommendations for improving the *Project Manager Competency Development Framework*—Second Edition:

Terry Andersen
Jennifer J. Atkinson, PMP
J. Chris Boyd, PMP
Patti Campbell, PMP
Frank Cox, MS, PMP
Wanda Curlee, PgMP, PMP
Edgardo J. Fitzpatrick, PMP
Robert G. Gagne, PMP
Alcides A. Gimenes, PMP
Leo A Giulianetti, PMP
Roy C. Greenia, PMP
Richard E. Hasz
George Hopman, PhD, PE
George Jackelen, PMP
Dorothy L. Kangas, PMP
Ramakrishna Kavirayani, PMP
Robert Bruce Kelsey, PhD
Ir Hj A Khairiri A Ghani, ASEAN Eng, Int. PE
JoAnn W. Klinedinst, PMP, FHIMSS
Timothy A. MacFadyen, MBA, PMP
Crispin "Kik" Piney, BSc, PMP
Paul Sanghera, PhD, PMP
K. S. Subrahmanyam, PMP

David J. Violette, MPM, PMP
Hao Wang, PhD, PMP
Jeffrey William White
Rebecca A. Winston, Esq

C5. PMI Project Management Standards Program Member Advisory Group

The following individuals served as members of the PMI Standards Program Member Advisory Group during development of the *Project Manager Competency Development Framework*—Second Edition:

Julia M. Bednar, PMP
Douglas Clark
Terry Cooke-Davies, PhD, BA
Carol Holliday, PMP
Thomas Kurihara
Debbie O'Bray
Asbjorn Rolstadas, PhD, Ing
David Ross, PMP
Cynthia Stackpole, PMP
Bobbye Underwood, PMP
David J. Violette, MPM, PMP

C6. PMI Staff

Special mention is due to the following employees of PMI:

Steve Fahrenkrog, PMP, Director, Knowledge Delivery Group
Dan Goldfischer, Editor-in-Chief
Ruth Anne Guerrero, PMP, former Standards Manager
Donn Greenberg, Manager, Publications
M. Elaine Lazar, Standards Project Specialist
John T. Roecker, EdD, Career Framework Manager
Roberta Storer, Product Editor
Kristin L. Vitello, Standards Project Specialist
Barbara Walsh, Publications Planner
Nan Wolfslayer, Standards Project Specialist

References

Crawford, L.H. 1997. A global approach to project management competence. *Proceedings of the 1997 AIPM National Conference, Gold Coast*, Brisbane: AIPM, 220–228.

Project Management Institute. 2005. *Project Manager Professional (PMP®) Examination Spec*. Newtown Square, PA: Project Management Institute.

Project Management Institute. *A Guide to the Project Management Body of Knowledge (PMBOK® Guide)—Third Edition*. Newtown Square, PA: Project Management Institute.

Roecker, J.T. 2005. *PMI's Career Framework: The case for a project manager path*. Newtown Square, PA: Project Management Institute.

Additional References

Aguinis, H. and Kraiger, K.T. April 1997. Practicing what we preach: Competency-based assessment of industrial/organizational psychology graduate students. *The Industrial-Organizational Psychologist*, 34–39.

Association for Project Management. The 40 key competencies. http://www.apmgroup.co.uk/apmbok.htm. Australian Institute of Project Management (AIPM). 1996. *National Competency Standards for Project Management*. Split Junction, NSW.

Anastasi, A. 1988. *Psychological Testing, 6th ed*. New York: Macmillan.

Bacharach, S.B. 1989. Organizational theories: Some criteria for evaluation. *Academy of Management Review, 14*(4), 496–515.

Belout, A. 1997. Effects of human resource management on project effectiveness and success: toward a new conceptual framework. *International Journal of Project Management, 16*(1). 21–26.

Boyatzis, R.E. 1982. *The competent manager: A model for effective performance*. New York: John Wiley & Sons.

Cascio, W.F. 1992. *Managing human resources: Productivity, quality of work life, profits*, 3rd Ed. New York: McGraw-Hill.

Crawford, L.H. 1998. Project management competence for strategy realisation. *Proceedings of the 14th World Congress on Project Management*. Ljubljana, Slovenia, *1*, 10–21.

Project Management Institute. 1999. Assessing and developing project management competence. *Proceedings of the 30th Annual Project Management Institute 1999 Seminars & Symposium*. Newtown Square, PA: Project Management Institute.

Dale, M. and Iles, P. 1992. *Assessing management skills: A guide to competencies and evaluation techniques*. London: Kogan.

Finn, R. 1993. A synthesis of current research on management competencies. Henly Working Paper HWP9310. Henley-on-Thames, Henley Management College.

Gadeken, O.C. (January-February 1997) Project Managers as Leaders: Competencies of Top Performers, *Army RD&A Magazine*, 2–7.

Gonczi, A., Hager, P. and Athanasou, J. 1993. *The development of competency-based assessment strategies for the professions*. Canberra: Australian Government Publishing Service.

Hellriegel, D. Slocum J.W., Jr., and Woodman, R.W. 1992. *Organizational Behavior, 6th Ed.* St. Paul: West.

Heneman, H.G., III, and Heneman, R.L. 1994. *Staffing Organizations.* Middleton: Mendota House.

Heywood, L., Gonczi, A. and Hager, P. 1992. *A Guide to Development of Competency Standards for Professionals.* Canberra: Australian Government Publishing Service.

Kleinmuntz, B. 1985. *Personality and Psychological Assessment.* Malabar: Robert E. Krieger.

McLagan, P.A. May 1997 Competencies: The next generation, *Training & Development, 51,* 40–47.

McClelland, D.C. January 1973). Testing for competence rather than for "intelligence," *American Psychologist* 1–14.

McVeigh, B.J. January-February 1995. The right stuff revisited: A competency perspective of army program managers, *Program Manager,* 30–34

Mealiea, L.W. and Latham, G.P. 1996. *Skills for managerial success: Theory, experience, and practice.* Chicago, IL: Irwin

Messick, S. November 1980. Test validity and the ethics of assessment. *American Psychologist, 35*(11) 1012–1027.

Mirabile, R.J. August 1997. Everything you wanted to know about competency modeling. *Training & Development, 51*(8) 73–77.

Morris, P.W.G. 1999. Body Building. Paper presented on project management forum (www.pmforum.org/digest/newapr99.htm).

NASA. Academy of Program/Project Leadership (formally called "NASA's Program/Project Management Initiative"). http://www.msfc.nasa.gov/training/PPMI/HOME.html.

Parry, S.B. 1998. Just What Is a Competency? (And Why Should You Care?) *Training,* (June), 58–64.

Pinto, J.K., and Slevin, D.P. February 1988. Project success: Definitions and measurement techniques, *Journal of Project Management, 19* (1), 67–72.

Posner, B.Z. 1987). What it takes to be a good project manager. *Project Management Journal,* March 1987. Newtown Square, PA: Project Management Institute.

Project Management Institute. 2000. *Project Management Professional (PMP) Role Delineation Study.* Newtown Square, PA: Project Management Institute.

Project Management Institute. 2000. *Project management experience and knowledge self-assessment manual.* Newtown Square, PA: Project Management Institute.

Skulmoski, G. June 1999. New locks and keys: Is cost engineering ready to contribute? *Presented at 43rd Annual Meeting of AACE International.*

Spencer, L.M., Jr., and Signe, M.S. 1993. *Competence at work: Models for superior performance.* New York: John Wiley & Sons.

Struckenbruck, L.C. 1986. Who determine project success? *PMI Seminar/Symposium Proceedings,* 85–93.

Thamhain, H.J., and Wilemon, D.L. 1982. Developing project/program managers. PMI Seminar/Symposium Proceedings, II-B.1–II-B.10.

Toney, F. July 1998. The quest to find the superior project manager: The Fortune 500 project management benchmarking forum defines competencies. *PM Network.* Newtown Square, PA.: Project Management Instutute.

Treasury Board of Canada Secretariat. An enhanced framework for the management of information technology projects—Project management core competencies. http://www.tbs-sct.gc.ca/cio-dpi/default.asp.

Ulrich, D., Brockbank, W., Yeung, A. K., & Lake, D. G. (Winter 1995). Human resource competencies: An empirical assessment. *Human Resource Management, 34*(4), 473–495.

U.S. Department of Defense. Project performance measurement standards. http://www.acq.osd.mil/pm/.

Waller, R. 1997. A Project Manager Competency Model. *Proceedings of the 28th Annual Project Management Institute 1997 Seminars & Symposium.* Newtown Square, PA: Project Management Institute.

Glossary

This glossary includes terms that are used in the *PMCD Framework*. These terms are not unique to project manager competence, but may be used differently or with a narrower meaning than that of general everyday usage.

Ability. The quality of being able to do something; the physical, mental, financial, or legal power to perform; a natural or acquired skill or talent.

Accept. The act of formally receiving or acknowledging something and regarding it as being true, sound, suitable, or complete.

Acceptance. See *accept*

Activity. A component of work performed during the course of a project.

Assumptions. Assumptions are factors that, for planning purposes, are considered to be true, real, or certain without proof or demonstration. Assumptions affect all aspects of project planning, and are part of the progressive elaboration of the project. Project teams frequently identify, document, and validate assumptions as part of their planning process. Assumptions generally involve a degree of risk.

Attitudes. Relatively lasting feelings, beliefs, and behavior tendencies directed toward specific persons, groups, ideas, issues, or objects. They are often described in terms of three components: (*a*) an affective component,or the feelings, sentiments, moods, and emotions about some person, idea, event, or object; (*b*) a cognitive component or the beliefs, opinions, knowledge, or information held by the individual; and (*c*) a behavioral component or the intention and predisposition to act.

Baseline. The approved time phased plan (for a project, a work breakdown structure component, a work package, or a schedule activity), plus or minus approved project scope, cost, schedule, and technical changes. Generally refers to the current baseline, but may refer to the original or some other baseline. Usually used with a modifier (e.g., cost baseline, schedule baseline, performance measurement baseline, technical baseline).

Behavior. The manner in which an individual acts or conducts oneself under specified circumstances.

Capability. A specific organization project management maturity (*OPM3*®) competency that must exist in order for an organization to execute project management processes and deliver project management services and products. Capabilities are incremental steps leading up to one or more Best Practices.

Change Control. Identifying, documenting, approving or rejecting, and controlling changes to the project baseline.

Change Control Board (CCB). A formally constituted group of stakeholders responsible for reviewing, evaluating, approving, delaying, or rejecting changes to the project, with all decisions and recommendations being recorded.

Change Request. Requests to expand or reduce the project scope, modify policies, processes, plans, or procedures, modify costs or budgets, or revise schedules. Requests for a change can be direct or indirect, externally or internally initiated, and legally or contractually mandated or optional. Only formally documented requested changes are processed and only approved change requests are implemented.

Communication. A process through which information is exchanged among persons using a common system of symbols, signs, or behaviors.

Communication Management Plan [Output/Input]. The document that describes: the communications needs and expectations for the project; how and in what format information will be communicated; when and where each communication will be made; and who is responsible for providing each type of communication. A communication management plan can be formal or informal, highly detailed or broadly framed, based on the requirements of the project stakeholders. The communication management plan is contained in, or is a subsidiary plan of, the project management plan.

Competence. A cluster of related knowledge, attitudes, skills, and other personal characteristics that affects a major part of one's job (i.e., one or more key roles or responsibilities), correlates with performance on the job, can be measured against well-accepted standards, and can be improved by means of training and development.

Major components of competencies include:

- Abilities
- Attitudes

- Behavior
- Knowledge
- Personality
- Skills

Major dimensions of competency include Knowledge Competence, Personal Competence, and Performance Competence.

See also *Knowledge Competence*, *Personal Competence*, and *Performance Competence*

Competence Baseline. An initial assessment of the individual compared to the personal Knowledge, Performance, and Personal Competencies as described in the *PMCD Framework*.

Competence Development Plan. A plan that prescribes activities to be undertaken by the project manager that are necessary to achieve the learning required after an assessment is performed to determine the competence gap.

Competence Dimensions. A multidimensional framework that breaks competency into dimensions of Knowledge, Performance and Personal Competencies.

Competence Gap. The difference between the desired level of competence within a given dimension and the level of competence assessed for an individual. It is the ''gaps'' in one's competence that an individual aims to improve through individual development.

Competency. See *Competence*

Cost Management Plan [Output/Input]. The document that sets out the format and establishes the activities and criteria for planning, structuring, and controlling the project costs. A cost management plan can be formal or informal, highly detailed or broadly framed, based on the requirements of the project stakeholders. The cost management plan is contained in, or is a subsidiary plan, of the project management plan.

Document. A medium and the information recorded thereon, that generally has permanence and can be read by a person or a machine. Examples include project management plans, specifications, procedures, studies, and manuals.

Effective Performance. An intended or expected accomplishment.

Elements of Competence. The basic building blocks of a Unit of Competence. They describe, in output terms, actions or outcomes, which are demonstrable and assessable.

Emotional Intelligence. Describes an ability, capacity, or skill to perceive, assess, and manage the emotions of one's self, of others, and of groups.

Feedback. A reaction or response to a particular process or activity.

Integrated Change Control [Process]. The process of reviewing all change requests, approving changes and controlling changes to deliverables and organizational process assets.

Knowledge. Knowing something with the familiarity gained through experience, education, observation, or investigation, it is understanding a process, practice, or technique, or how to use a tool.

Knowledge Competence. The knowledge and understanding that a project manager brings to a project. This can include qualifications and experience, both direct and related. These are the knowledge components of competence.

Lessons Learned [Output/Input]. The learning gained from the process of performing the project. Lessons learned may be identified at any point. Also considered a project record, to be included in the lessons learned knowledge base.

Organizational Process Assets [Output/Input]. Any or all process related assets, from any or all of the organizations involved in the project that are or can be used to influence the project's success. These process assets include formal and informal plans, policies, procedures, and guidelines. The process assets also include the organizations' knowledge bases such as lessons learned and historical information.

Outcome. The tangible or intangible result of applying a capability.

Performance Criteria. An integrated list of aspects of performance that would be regarded as displaying competent performance during a project in an element of competence.

Performance Competence. What the project manager is able to do or accomplish by applying project management knowledge. This competency dimension looks at the demonstrable performance of the individual in carrying out project management tasks, and focuses on the project outcomes grouped in five units: Initiating, Planning, Executing, Monitoring and Controlling, and Closing a Project.

Personality. A unique organization of a relatively stable set of characteristics, tendencies, and temperaments that define an individual and determine that person's interaction with the environment.

Personal Competence. The core personality characteristics underlying a person's capability to do a project. These are the behavior, motives, traits, attitudes, and self-concepts that enable a person to successfully manage a project, grouped into six units: communicating, leading, managing, cognitive ability, effectiveness, and professionalism.

Procurement Management Plan. The document that describes how procurement processes from developing procurement documentation through contract closure will be managed.

Project Charter [Output/Input]. A document issued by the project initiator or sponsor that formally authorizes the existence of a project, and provides the project manager with the authority to apply organizational resources to project activities.

Project Management (PM). The application of knowledge, skills, tools, and techniques to project activities to meet the project requirements.

Project Performance. A measure of the extent to which the project is carried out as planned in terms of objectives, time and financial constraints, and organizational policies and procedures.

Project Schedule [Output/Input]. The planned dates for performing schedule activities and the planned dates for meeting schedule milestones.

Project Success. A collective assessment by project stakeholders (e.g., client/customer, sponsor) of the degree to which the project has achieved each of its objectives.

Quality Management Plan [Output/Input]. The quality management plan describes how the project management team will implement the performing organization's quality policy. The quality management plan is a component or a subsidiary plan of the project management plan. The quality management plan may be formal or informal, highly detailed, or broadly framed, based on the requirements of the project.

Responsibility Assignment Matrix (RAM) [Tool]. A structure that relates the project *organizational breakdown structure* to the *work breakdown structure* to help ensure that each component of the project's *scope* of *work* is assigned to a responsible person/team

Risk Management Plan [Output/Input]. The document describing how project risk management will be structured and performed on the project. It is contained in or is a subsidiary plan of the project management plan. The risk management plan can be informal and broadly framed, or formal and highly detailed, based on the needs of the project. Information in the risk management plan varies by application area and project size. The risk management plan is different from the risk register that contains the list of project risks, the results of risk analysis, and the risk responses.

Risk Mitigation [Technique]. A risk response planning technique associated with threats that seeks to reduce the probability of occurrence or impact of a risk to below an acceptable threshold.

Risk Register [Output/Input]. The document containing the results of the qualitative risk analysis, quantitative risk analysis, and risk response planning. The risk register details all identified risks, including description, category, cause, probability of occurring, impact(s) on objectives, proposed responses, owners, and current status. The risk register is a component of the project management plan.

Risk Response Planning [Process]. The process of developing options and actions to enhance opportunities and to reduce threats to project objectives.

Seller. A provider or supplier of products, services, or results to an organization.

Skill. Ability to use knowledge, a developed aptitude, and/or a capability to effectively and readily execute or perform an activity.

Staffing Management Plan [Output/Input]. The document that describes when and how human resource requirements will be met. It is contained in, or is a subsidiary plan of, the project management plan. The staffing management plan can be informal and broadly framed, or formal and highly detailed, based on the needs of the project. Information in the staffing management plan varies by application area and project size.

Stakeholder. Person or organization (e.g., customer, sponsor, performing organization or the public) that is actively involved in the project, or whose interests may be positively or negatively affected by execution or completion of the project. A stakeholder may also exert influence over the project and its deliverables.

Style. A set of skills, attributes, or characteristics of a person; the concept refers to a frequent pattern of what is said, done, expressed, or performed by a person demonstrating one's values. It encompasses the modes or patterns of behavior that people exhibit in approaching their work and interacting with others.

Subject Matter Expert (SME). A person, usually an accomplished performer, who knows the knowledge, performance, and personal competence required for a given Unit of Competence.

360° Feedback. The type of feedback in which project team members, project sponsors, and other stakeholders are surveyed anonymously in regard to the project manager's performance. This can be used to assess baseline competence in order to complete a competence gap analysis and create a development or training plan.

Types of Evidence. Specific documented proof that Performance Criteria are achieved or expected action has been completed; these form the basis upon which competence can be assessed.

Unit of Competence. A major segment of overall competency, typically representing a major function.

Work Breakdown Structure (WBS) [Output/Input]. A deliverable-oriented hierarchical decomposition of the work to be executed by the project team to accomplish the project objectives and create the required deliverables. It organizes and defines the total scope of the project. Each descending level represents an increasingly detailed definition of the project work. The WBS is decomposed into work packages. The deliverable orientation of the hierarchy includes both internal and external deliverables.

Work Breakdown Structure Dictionary [Output/Input]. A document that describes each component in the work breakdown structure (WBS). For each WBS component, the WBS dictionary includes a brief definition of the scope or statement of work, defined deliverable(s), a list of associated activities, and a list of milestones. Other information may include: responsible organization, start and end dates, resources required, an estimate of cost, charge number, contract information, quality requirements, and technical references to facilitate performance of the work.

Index

W